Regional Futures
and Transatlantic
Economic Relations

Miles Kahler

Published for the
European Community Studies Association

COUNCIL ON FOREIGN RELATIONS PRESS

NEW YORK

COUNCIL ON FOREIGN RELATIONS BOOKS

*If you would like more information on Council publications, please write
the Council on Foreign Relations, 58 East 68th Street, New York, NY
10021, or call the Publications Office at (212)734-0400.*

Library of Congress Cataloging-in-Publication Data

Kahler, Miles, 1949–
    Regional futures and transatlantic economic relations / by Miles Kahler.
        p.   cm.
    "Published for the European Community Studies Association."
    Includes bibliographical references and index.
    ISBN 0-87609-182-6 (paper)
    1. United States—Foreign economic relations—European Union countries.
2. European Union countries—Foreign economic relations—United States.
3. Environmental policy—United States.   4. Environmental policy—European
Union countries.   I. European Community Studies Association.   II. Title
    HF1456.EBK34   1995
    337.7304—dc20   95–41303
                                                                        CIP

95   96   97   98   99   EB   10   9   8   7   6   5   4   3   2   1

Cover Design: Dorothy Wachtenheim

Regional Futures and Transatlantic Economic Relations

CONTENTS

FOREWORD

The European Community Studies Association (ECSA) presents its second biennial United States–European Union Relations Project publication with this work by Professor Miles Kahler. Whereas the first publication, Dr. Catherine Kelleher's *A New Security Order: The United States and the European Community in the 1990s*, focused on the dimension of the transatlantic relationship historically rooted in the Cold War, this work focuses on the economic dimension, newly important since the end of the Cold War. "Regional futures" are central to the evolving transatlantic relationship as is the question of how they will relate to the multilateral economic institutions, which are themselves also in transition.

In the publication presented here, the Executive Committee of the European Community Studies Association feels especially fortunate in having Professor Miles Kahler as the author. Miles Kahler has published distinguished work on both European and Asian affairs, and thus was uniquely qualified to research the topic that the Executive Committee chose as the successor to Dr. Kelleher's work. The originality and power of Professor Kahler's work confirm our initial view that his analysis would make an important contribution to the ongoing debate about transatlantic economic relations.

The US-EU Relations Project is a most unusual one. It involves the choosing of a topic and the commissioning of a prominent scholar by ECSA's Executive Committee, the presentation of the author's first draft to meetings of experts in Washington, D.C., and Brussels, the delivery of the final version in a plenary session at ECSA's Biennial Conference (held this year in Charleston, South Carolina), and, finally, publication. Generous financial support is critical for such an ambitious project. ECSA is grateful to The German Marshall Fund of the United States, DGI (External Affairs) of the Commission of the European Community, and to the Trans-European Policy Studies Association for their assistance.

The analysis and conclusion presented by Miles Kahler have been formulated through interaction with an unusually stimulating and expert audience. The core of the US-EU Relations Project involves the presentation of the author's original draft to knowledgeable Americans and Europeans who critique the manuscript. The author's published version therefore incorporates the insights of a varied group of American and European researchers, policymakers, representatives of nongovernmental organizations, and journalists.

ECSA would like to thank C. Randall Henning (Institute for International Economics), Michael Froman (National Economic Council), Mary Saunders (National Institute of Standards and Technology, U.S. Department of Commerce), Hilary French (Worldwatch Institute), Thea Lea (Economic Policy Institute), Willard Berry (European-American Chamber of Commerce), and Wolfgang Reinicke (The Brookings Institution) for their insightful comments and criticisms at the January 1995 meeting in Washington, D.C. For the March 1995 meeting in Brussels, ECSA was fortunate in cooperating with the Trans-European Policy Studies Association (TEPSA). Both TEPSA's outgoing chair—Professor Jacques Vandamme—and incoming chair—Professor Wolfgang Wessels—were most helpful in ensuring the success of the Brussels meeting. Professor Theo Peters (Catholic University of Leuven), Mr. Dick Hudig (ICI Group), Mr. Ove Juul Jorgensen (DGI of the European Commission), Professor

E.L.M. Volker (University of Amsterdam), and Ms. Sandrine Dixson-Declève (Environmental Policy Centre Europe) incisively critiqued Professor Kahler's draft, and their suggestions improved the final version.

ECSA is also indebted to the work of the subcommittee that worked so hard to organize the Washington and Brussels meetings. James Caporaso (University of Washington), the subcommittee's chair, Lily Gardner Feldman (American Institute for Contemporary German Studies), and Carl Lankowski (American University) have been critical to the success of the project. Bill Burros, ECSA's administrative director, has contributed in innumerable ways to this project from its conception.

I, as outgoing chair of ECSA's Executive Committee, and James Caporaso, incoming chair, would both like to thank all of those who have helped make this second US-EU Relations Project such a success. We hope that this publication will prove useful in both the classroom and in policy circles, and we are delighted to cooperate with the Council on Foreign Relations to bring Professor Kahler's work to both audiences.

Alberta Sbragia
Director, Center for West European Studies
University of Pittsburgh
June 1995

ACKNOWLEDGMENTS

The European Community Studies Association is a unique organization—a scholarly association with strong interests in contemporary policy issues, a genuinely transatlantic forum for those who are investigating the European Union. I was honored by the ECSA's invitation to become the second author in the ECSA US-EU Relations Project. The plan of the project was imaginative and invaluable in improving the quality of this work. I am indebted to Alberta R. Sbragia, chair of the ECSA Executive Committee, to the members of the ECSA Executive Committee, to Bill Burros, administrative director, and to the members of ECSA for supporting this project.

I am also grateful to the Council on Foreign Relations, its president, Leslie H. Gelb, and its senior vice president for programs, Kenneth H. Keller. Although I accepted the ECSA invitation before joining the Council as senior fellow for international political economy, the Council provided an excellent site for exploring transatlantic economic relations. David Kellogg, director of publications, has overseen a timely publication in collaboration with the ECSA. Patricia Dorff, managing editor, and Miriam Familia-Garcia, production assistant, were central to the successful editing and production of this book.

Discussants at the Washington and Brussels conferences provided valuable comments on earlier drafts of the manuscript. Benjamin J. Cohen, C. Randall Henning, John Peterson, and Tony Smith also gave detailed comments that improved the published version.

Timothy Johnson, program assistant at the Council on Foreign Relations, has been research assistant, travel organizer, and organizational liaison throughout this project. His extraordinary contribution of time and energy was essential to the successful completion of this study.

Miles Kahler
New York
June 6, 1995

INTRODUCTION

The Cold War deepened the transatlantic relationship, creating a dense military and economic fabric between the United States and Europe. The end of the Cold War has created anxiety about the resilience of that architecture in new international circumstances. Some observers endorse a simple realist position: no threat, no alliance (eventually). In some stark predictions the bipolar world of the Cold War and the firm frame that it provided for the Atlantic economies will be succeeded by a return to a more unstable and conflict-prone world of multipolarity.[1]

Since the NATO alliance was the centerpiece of the transatlantic relationship, fears of heightened economic conflict and institutional erosion have grown as well. Economic internationalists have portrayed a world economy that inevitably coalesces into regional blocs as one that will reduce economic prosperity through high barriers to trade and investment and lead to political and even military conflict. For those pessimistic about the potential for continued collaboration in a multipolar world economy, the end of the Cold War has eroded the last pillar of transatlantic economic cooperation: a future of conflicting blocs is at hand. Lester Thurow has painted this future in alarming fashion, using the terminology of economic warfare.[2] Others have argued that global multilateral institutions are unlikely to manage economic conflicts among Europe, the United States, and Japan in the absence of cohesion induced by the Cold War.[3]

These pessimistic predictions of future relations between the United States and Europe can be challenged on several grounds. One dimension of the new international setting is assumed to dominate all others: an end of the Soviet threat implies erosion of the Atlantic alliance, which in turn produces higher levels of economic conflict. Theoretically, the precise causal priority awarded security or economic relations is a contentious issue.[4] A careful reading of history before the Cold War demonstrates, however, that transatlantic economic relations combined collaboration and conflict before a military alliance was constructed to meet the Soviet threat. The United States was not disengaged economically from Europe in those earlier decades; it was deeply engaged in a program of government-supported private diplomacy.[5] The Cold War alliance also *produced* economic conflicts as well as suppressing them. Different readings of the Soviet threat and conflicting economic strategies toward the Soviet bloc led to repeated arguments and crises over the export control regime. West European reactions were sharp and unified when the United States attempted to extend extraterritorial controls in an effort to stop the Siberian gas pipeline in 1981–82. The dissolution of the Soviet bloc has returned many, if not all, such issues to the realm of economic competition rather than alliance politics.

Just as more alarmist accounts of contemporary alliance relations have overlooked the contribution of the Cold War to transatlantic discord, the post-1945 international economy also provided sources of conflict that have now dissipated. Apart from Cold War–induced conflicts over strategy toward the Soviet Union, many of the sharpest alliance crises were caused by rivalry between the United States and Europe in the developing world. During and after decolonization, disagreements over Middle Eastern policy, colored by petroleum politics, were recurrent. In the 1970s the United States and Europe competed even more intensely for export markets and resources. One key change in the international economy during the 1980s and 1990s has been a steady decline in the price of most commodities, including petroleum: a burden for exporters of those raw materials but a boon for transatlantic relations. Competition for secure supplies of key resources and politicized competition for the markets of resource exporters have enjoyed a parallel decline.

An overly nostalgic view of the Cold War era can lead to flawed prescriptions for the future. Excessive concentration on one feature of the international environment—however dramatic—may lead to a deceptively monocausal view of the future. The Cold War's end coincided with other developments that may prove to be equally important for the future of the international economy. The widening of economic integration beyond the industrialized economies is perhaps the most striking. Developing and socialist countries have embraced market-oriented policies and opening to the international economy. Associated with this process of integration, regional arrangements have proliferated in both the industrialized and developing worlds. The first change was only partly related to the collapse of the Soviet empire—many non-communist and some communist states began their programs of economic reform much earlier. The rapid growth of new and revived regional arrangements began before the East-West divide had disappeared and continues in the 1990s. Viewing this regional activism solely through the lens of the 1930s and the end of the Cold War has situated it incorrectly. The principal sources of regionalization and regional institution-building are not the defensive ones of earlier decades. Nevertheless, regionalization may have implications for transatlantic relations as powerful as changes in the strategic environment.

The following investigation of the effects of regionalism on relations between the United States and Europe begins with an outline of the dynamics of regionalization in the 1990s, an essential prerequisite for any assessment of its implications for transatlantic relations. Three dimensions of regionalism that are likely to affect economic relations between the United States and the European Union are considered in the following sections. A decade ago, any consideration of regional projects and their effect on the economic relations between the United States and Europe would have dealt with only one side of the Atlantic: the European Community. Transatlantic conflict was associated with American ambivalence in its embrace of European integration. For reasons of alliance burden-sharing and mobilizing resources against the Soviet Union, the United States supported Europe's regional experiment, but its suspicions of the discriminatory effects of integration on global economic regimes persisted. Now the United States has its own regional projects in North America, the Western Hemisphere, and the Pacific. Although these do not yet display the institutional weight of the EU, they have meant that the United States will no longer act solely on bilateral and global levels: regional instruments are now at hand. How this new regional dimension will influence American foreign economic policy and particularly its economic stance toward Europe is the subject of the second section of this work.

The European half of regional evolution is of equal importance. Whether defined as nation-states pooling sovereignty or a proto-federation, institution-building in the EU is more advanced than any other regional entity. For most of its history, the institutional design of the European Community was not of central concern to outsiders, since the competences of the Community were narrow and the weight of its institutions was relatively light. Following the Single European Act and the Maastricht Treaty, however, institutional architecture may have significant consequences for those outside the EU. This peculiar international actor displays a high degree of delegated authority from its member nations and growing problems of coordination as it enlarges. The EU could, on one view, provide a model for organizing national and subnational units to deal with the rest of the world. Other architectural choices, however, could present its interlocutors with a cumbersome and unpredictable partner in perpetual transition. The consequences of European institution-building for the United States and transatlantic economic relations are explored in the third section.

Finally, regionalization could intersect with the new agenda of international economic relations in a way that drives the United States and Europe apart. Points of economic conflict could coalesce into a clash of systems, and regional entities, even if relatively liberal in their external orientation, could grate against one another. Increasingly the points of conflict among the industrialized countries are not the familiar ones of barriers to exchange at the border, but an entire array of "domestic" policies that produce conflict by appearing to restrict market access or alter the terms of competition. The agenda of behind-the-border issues that has become more prominent in the 1990s will only grow as economic integration continues and groups mobilize to seek new benchmarks for an international "level playing field." Whether the economic issues that divide the United States and the European Union are congealing into system friction could mean the difference between incremental and successful management on previous models or cumulative and reinforcing lines of cleavage with graver consequences for the economic relationship.

The prophets of bloc warfare do not aid in clear thinking about the implications of regionalism in the last decade of the twentieth century. Regional futures remain open, as does the future of the global economy that must accommodate them. For every dire warning of closure and discrimination, one can paint an equally convincing assessment of regions that manage their internal and external relations in a cooperative and efficient way. Recent calls for safeguarding economic collaboration between the United States and Eu-

rope have included proposals to institutionalize the transatlantic region in the form of a free trade agreement, a common
"economic area," or a new treaty. The final section evaluates
these strategies and others that lie before the European Union
and the United States in managing their economic relations,
given the changing international setting of the Atlantic political economy. A keener sense of the externalities of regional
initiatives and the fit between those initiatives and global institutions may encourage regional outcomes that have benign
effects on both transatlantic and global futures.

REGIONALISM IN THE 1990s

The new regionalism of the 1990s bears little resemblance to
earlier waves of interest in regional organization of the world
economy.[6] Four characteristics make it unlikely that the current explosion of regional arrangements is either a short-lived
international fad or a precursor of conflictual and closed
blocs. Regionalism is based on economic realities: political
regionalism has followed the emergence of economic regions. The dominance of economic regionalism has produced less formal institution-building and considerable
variation in regional institutions. Rather than transferring national protectionism to a larger sphere, contemporary regionalism is set in a liberalizing environment and grounded
in a shift toward economic opening and market-oriented policies. Finally, behind-the-border issues that have risen on the
international economic agenda during the past decade are included in many regional arrangements. In this respect regional agreements have been able to innovate more rapidly
than the global trade regime.

   Any discussion of regionalism in the contemporary international economy must distinguish at the outset between
economic (or "soft") regionalism and political (or "hard")

regionalism.[7] Although international economic transactions never take place in a political vacuum, economic regionalism—based on the independent and market-driven decisions of private traders, investors, and workers—is distinguishable from a redirection of economic transactions as the result of conscious political decisions and formal international agreements. The degree of intraregional trade bias in East Asia and in the Pacific, for example, is greater than would be expected on the basis of simple proximity, even though there is no intergovernmental framework to encourage that trade. (Political *changes* in the region, such as the end of China's isolation from the regional economy, may have had a significant influence on the further development of such biases.) Among the three large regions in the international economy—Asia-Pacific, Europe, the Western Hemisphere—the last two demonstrated an increase in intraregional trade bias during the 1980s. Only Europe displayed "hard" regional arrangements, although the Canada–United States Trade Agreement (CUSTA) may have influenced the results in the Western Hemisphere.[8]

When foreign direct investment is added to the pattern of integration, both measurement and implications for future economic interconnection become more complex. In East Asia, currency realignments after 1985 spurred intraregional investment flows and the growth in production networks in a number of sectors; both Japanese and NIC (newly industrializing country) investment surged during this period. Adding this new layer to economic regionalism is likely to intensify intraregional trade flows and may stimulate a new economic agenda driven by the demands of investors. The deepening of sectoral investment links in Asia also may create a hybrid, "semisoft" regionalism: informal government-business links that may favor regional investors over those from outside the region, even in the absence of formal intergovernmental arrangements. [9]

Economic regionalism has been more prevalent than political regionalism in the past decade. Although stimulated in part by closer economic integration in Europe under the Single European Act, new regional arrangements seldom mimic the institutional design of the European Union.[10] Nor is there conclusive evidence that intensifying economic integration leads in any clear-cut fashion toward the elaboration of regional institutions. Economic relations between the United States and Canada deepened for decades before a formal free trade agreement was concluded; regional and subregional nodes in Asia-Pacific have developed without institutional support and occasionally in the presence of positive hostility between governments (China and Taiwan, for example). A high degree of institutional variation and, in some regions, a reluctance to endorse more formal institutional arrangements seem to characterize the latest phase of regionalization.

The motivations that drive formal regional arrangements also help to explain the relatively low level of institutionalization associated with contemporary regionalism. Developing countries used regionalism to reinforce import-substituting strategies three decades ago; in the 1990s regional arrangements often confirm a shift toward outward orientation. As a result, many of the new arrangements include both industrialized and developing countries. Rather than efforts to enlarge a protected economic space, two motivations drive developing countries toward regional arrangements: on the one hand, a desire to lock in and lend credibility to relatively recent shifts in economic policy toward opening and liberalization, and, on the other, an effort to protect market access in the large industrialized economies. Market access is threatened less by systemic protectionism than by the arbitrary and unpredictable use of administrative trade measures. For industrialized countries, expanding market access in rapidly growing economies and reinforcing liberal economic policies remain prime motivations.

Even the General Agreement on Tariffs and Trade (GATT), which has every reason to be skeptical of regional trade arrangements, has accepted that regionalization in the 1990s takes place in a liberalizing environment, is often based on initial unilateral liberalizations, and can reinforce further steps in external opening.[11] Such broadly liberal motivations for "harder" regional arrangements do not mean that their liberalism is unadulterated, however. Even if border protection remains constant or decreases as the result of a regional trade agreement, rules of origin, regional content requirements, and other less obvious nontariff barriers to trade and investment can make regional free trade agreements (FTAs) "protection friendly." In addition, political pressures to maintain existing levels of regulation in the interest of "good" public ends—such as environmental protection or consumer safety—may result in the incorporation of disguised protection in regional agreements. [12]

Finally, although regionalization that begins to "harden" into formal agreements and international obligations often takes the form of a free trade agreement, the new agenda of many regional arrangements extends well beyond the traditional goal of lowering or eliminating tariff barriers. As economist Robert Lawrence has pointed out, and as experience in each region has confirmed, much of the pressure for regional liberalization comes from corporations that are actual or prospective investors in the region. Their agenda of market access and national treatment (including right of establishment) extends well beyond even an expanded trade agenda.[13] A host of "domestic" regulatory structures may be subjected to international scrutiny because of their implications for market entry and their perceived effects on the competitive position of domestic and foreign firms.

The record of the new regionalism suggests that it has, on balance, contributed to global economic liberalization rather than undermining it. How it affects the policies of the two largest economic actors—the United States and the European Union—will determine whether it continues to have such benign effects.

THE UNITED STATES, REGIONAL PROJECTS, AND TRANSATLANTIC RELATIONS

The new regionalism that has emerged at the end of the twentieth century displays another striking distinction from regionalism in earlier decades. The United States, long attached to multilateral trade liberalization under the GATT and suspicious of the discriminatory implications of regional blocs, has become an enthusiastic promoter of and participant in regional and plurilateral trade initiatives over the last decade.[14] To understand the sources of this shift in American preferences and to assess its implications accurately, one must look to changes in American trade policy in the 1980s. The first Reagan administration implemented a macroeconomic policy mix that produced an overvalued dollar and a yawning current account deficit. At the same time, in the depths of the 1981–82 recession, the United States pressed an agenda for a new round of GATT negotiations that would deal with some of the weaknesses that it found in earlier GATT results. The European Community, which at that time took a skeptical stance toward the multilateral trade regime, firmly rebuffed those initiatives.

As the misalignment in exchange rates produced ever more intense pressure on American manufacturing and as demands for protection grew, the Reagan administration moved on several fronts in 1985. First, after many pronouncements against active intervention in the exchange markets, it switched to an active policy of macroeconomic coordination to bring down the value of the dollar. Second, it set out once again to begin GATT negotiations, a process that bore fruit with the opening of the Uruguay Round in September 1986. The administration also refurbished and extended its use of "aggressive unilateralism": measures that threatened trade retaliation to end "unfair" trade practices and force market opening. (This element in American trade policy is discussed at greater length later.) Finally, the United States negotiated a free trade agreement with Israel and opened negotiations for a Canada–United States Free Trade Agreement. With these steps, the United States made clear that further delays in multilateral liberalization and continued resistance to an expanded GATT agenda would lead it to advance its commercial interests in regional trade agreements.[15]

The American turn to regionalism in North America was conditioned on significant policy changes in its two regional trading partners—a decline in economic nationalism (removing restrictions on foreign direct investment as well as trade) and a concern over American unilateralism in the application of countervailing duties and antidumping levies. The United States soon developed its own rationale for such agreements: plurilateral negotiations permitted more efficient treatment of new agenda items—agriculture, services, and behind-the-border barriers to access—that the GATT was unable to address. Regional agreements became a means for the United States to push forward this "GATT-plus" agenda and increase its leverage in the Uruguay Round negotiations.

The Bush administration agenda of regional activism—negotiating the North American Free Trade Agreement (NAFTA), formulating the Enterprise for the Americas Initiative, and initiating Asia-Pacific Economic Cooperation (APEC)—has been adopted with even greater enthusiasm by the Clinton administration. Economic trends alone cannot fully explain this new turn. The United States, alone among the major industrialized countries, remains deeply and symmetrically engaged in three regions: Europe, Asia-Pacific, and Latin America. Although the relative importance of trade with East and Southeast Asia has grown in the past two decades, Europe still remains the most important site for American foreign direct investment, and the European Union is a principal American trading partner. The progress of economic reforms in Latin America and the acceleration of economic growth there after the debt crisis of the 1980s has led to a resurgence in American exports to the region, but its relative importance is still far less than in earlier decades.[16] Recent American investment in regional initiatives in both Latin America and the Pacific reflects more than an inevitable political consequence of the growing economic importance of these regions. A new element in U.S. foreign economic policy, these initiatives are uncharted and hard-to-predict features of future American policies toward Europe.

NAFTA and the Western Hemisphere

The negotiation of NAFTA with Canada and Mexico marked an important advance in the GATT-plus agenda that the United States favored in regional arrangements. In addition to a reduction in tariffs and nontariff barriers to trade in manufactures, NAFTA liberalizes agricultural trade, services, and investment.[17] NAFTA also includes a new dispute settlement model that uses binational panels to examine whether national laws and regulations governing antidumping and countervailing duties are applied as intended. Two side agreements covering environmental and labor standards adopted the same approach of international surveillance of national implementation. Those agreements extended the content of trade agreements into controversial new areas, but they aimed only at more rigorous enforcement of existing national standards, not explicit harmonization of national policies. In both dispute settlement mechanisms, very little pooling of sovereignty in the European sense was achieved:

resistance to supranationality was as great in the United States as in the other members.

The enthusiasm of Latin American states for concluding free trade agreements with the United States has been startling, given their historical suspicions of the North American giant and their long legacies of protectionism and economic nationalism. The Western Hemisphere states must now choose an appropriate path to closer integration among the economies of the region, a path that will link NAFTA and the many bilateral and plurilateral trade agreements in Central and South America. (The most significant of these is MERCOSUR, among Brazil, Argentina, Paraguay, and Uruguay.) The United States and many other governments in the region seem to favor accession to NAFTA as the model for hemispheric integration. Skeptics point out that the hurdles to accession will be high for most Latin American economies, since the United States will insist on environmental and labor side agreements. Another obstacle to this strategy is the "hardening" of MERCOSUR as a customs union and an alternative pole to NAFTA in the region. As a result, using NAFTA as the principal instrument for regional integration may produce a very differentiated multispeed agreement that could result in conflict between members and prospective members and higher transaction costs for outsiders.[18] Another option that has been proposed as a complement to a lengthy NAFTA-based process of integration: gradual multilateralization of existing subregional trade accords that threaten to complicate future hemispheric economic integration if they harden and become incompatible.[19]

The Summit of the Americas held in Miami in December 1994 endorsed creation of a Free Trade Area of the Americas by the year 2005. The proposed agreement will include liberalization commitments that move beyond trade to intellectual property, services, investment, and competition policy. The Clinton administration also has stipulated that labor and environmental side agreements must be part of an eventual FTAA. The fate of negotiations for Chile's accession to NAFTA will be an important bellwether of progress toward a hemispheric agreement. Two events—the Republican victories in the congressional elections of November 1994 and the Mexican financial crisis that began immediately after the Miami summit—have called into question rapid completion of either the Chilean negotiations or the FTAA. The insistence of Republican majorities in Congress that future hemispheric agreements omit environmental and labor accords threatens deadlock with the Democratic administration and congressional minority. The Mexican crisis has emboldened the opponents of NAFTA and increased popular and congressional skepticism toward any extension of the NAFTA template to other Latin American partners.

The Miami initiative leaves two key questions unanswered, given the lengthy time horizon for achieving hemispheric free trade. Each parallels—at a much earlier stage of economic integration—European experience. As economic integration proceeds, within and outside the original NAFTA, will members coordinate other external policies and will that coordination be accompanied by further institutionalization and "hardening" of the arrangement? Some accept a simple functionalist logic and posit that economic integration will imply institutional deepening over time.[20] On the other hand, resistance to encroachments on national sovereignty (already apparent in the NAFTA negotiations) suggest that further "hardening" is far from inevitable. Equally important for the European Union and those outside the Western Hemisphere is how rapidly other members of the hemisphere can be included and under what institutional format—any of the options just outlined suggest a multispeed process of widening that makes enlargement of the European Union to the east appear uncomplicated. Unless multilateral efforts are undertaken to harmonize the thicket of preferential agreements, the increase in transaction costs could be substantial in the medium term.

The Pacific and APEC

Latin America's embrace of economic integration with the United States is startling. The region's bargaining advantages and external options were clearly reduced by its debt crisis during the 1980s and by the fragile character of its economic reforms. For much of Pacific-Asia, economic success in the 1980s and 1990s—whether measured in export performance or in rates of growth—provides one explanation for a lack of interest in regional economic arrangements. The shift toward outward orientation (although not wholesale liberalization) in the region was carried out unilaterally, often by authoritarian or single-party governments that did not need to purchase credibility from external institutions. East and Southeast Asian economies performed very well in a postwar world of multilateral liberalization under the GATT. When coupled with unilateral and piecemeal opening of their national economies, regional initiatives seemed unnecessary.

On the other side of the Pacific, the United States at times pressed its East Asian allies to construct multilateral frameworks for security and economic collaboration. At other times, the United States seemed to prefer a bilateral, hub-and-spokes arrangement in the region, a design that maximized its bargaining advantages in trade disputes and secured military bases for its competition with the Soviet Union. In the 1980s regional initiatives were complicated by the rapid economic rise of Japan, opening the awkward issue of whether U.S. policy would dominate any Pacific grouping.

The formation of Asia-Pacific Economic Cooperation in 1989 marked a modest shift toward the same calculus that had spurred negotiation of regional arrangements in the Western Hemisphere. A trade-driven dynamic of growth became more dependent on foreign investment following revaluation of the yen and other East Asian currencies. GATT had just begun to address issues of investment as they related to trade; a regional organization might move more effectively. The developing countries in the region, particularly the members of the Association of Southeast Asian Nations (ASEAN), remained wary of a Pacific regional organization dominated by either the United States or Japan, but they also saw benefits in even modest guarantees of market access in the United States. As the Cold War in the Pacific faded, concern over the competition that regional initiatives might pose for alliance relations declined in the U.S. government. At the same time, concern grew in Asia over the means to maintain a U.S. security presence. Perhaps the most important motivation for APEC, however, was the need for an insurance policy should the Uruguay Round fail and the world economy slip into competing regional blocs. That concern appeared to tip the opponents and skeptics of Pacific institution-building toward the informal APEC alternative. Institutional ambition was not APEC's defining characteristic. Its first years were devoted to creating a Pacific lobby within the global trade talks and instituting a series of working groups that explored policy issues of joint concern.

The Clinton administration has taken a much more activist stance within APEC, pressing for the organization to become a focus for regional economic integration rather than a weak regional version of the Organization for Economic Cooperation and Development (OECD). The first APEC summit (Seattle, 1993) demonstrated to some observers that the organization had become "a negotiating forum rather than a purely consultative body."[21] Although the summit had been presented with an ambitious report by its Eminent Persons Group (EPG), however, its principal accomplishment was agreement on a common negotiating position for the endgame of the Uruguay Round trade negotiations.[22] The future of APEC became a bargaining chip with the European Union in the GATT negotiations: failure to agree to a new global accord could be met by deepening the American-led process of integration in the fastest growing region of the world economy. The APEC leaders authorized little else beyond existing working groups, although the consultative process was widened (to include regular meetings of finance ministers, for example).

The second APEC summit (Bogor, Indonesia, November 1994) went further toward constructing a program for regionwide liberalization. Consonant with the second EPG report (August 1994), the summit not only agreed to a long-term goal of "free and open trade and investment" in the Asia-Pacific region, it also approved a nonbinding set of principles to govern investment.[23] The liberalization timetable was lengthy and multispeed: industrialized countries by 2010 and developing countries by 2020. Although the summit commitment clearly included investment, it was ambiguous on many points—whether services as well as goods would be liberalized, to what degree agriculture was included, and which countries were "developing." Nevertheless, a clear commitment had been taken at the highest political level to a GATT-plus agenda of liberalization that went well beyond removal of barriers to trade at the border, incorporating harmonization of standards and a review of competition policies. A detailed blueprint was requested for the 1995 summit in Osaka. Despite ambiguities in the declaration, the degree of consensus reached and the willingness to accept a timetable for liberalization—however far it stretched into the future—was unexpected to many who had observed APEC's short history. ("Frankly amazing" was the observation of Hong Kong's financial secretary.)

Despite this unexpected progress on the road from consultative talking shop to free trade agreement, APEC's evolution is likely to be slow for several reasons. The consensus forged at Bogor was thin. For some time Prime Minister Mohamad Mahathir of Malaysia has pressed his alternative to APEC, an East Asian Economic Caucus that would exclude the United States. At the summit, he declared that liberalization commitments were "nonbinding" and the timetable "indicative."[24] China, although less vocal than Malaysia, made clear its own reservations about liberalization in this regional forum. More significantly, even those governments in Asia that endorsed the liberalization goals of APEC voiced reservations about the path toward those goals that the United States and Australia were pressing for. A choice of either the Asian or the American strategy will have significant consequences for the future evolution of APEC and for the interests of the European Union and others that remain outside the group.

The second EPG report and the summit declaration were unclear on the content of "open regionalism," since the American and Asian (particularly Japanese) definitions diverged. For the United States, open regionalism meant that liberalization within APEC should be extended to nonmembers on a conditional most-favored-nation basis. Implicitly, such reciprocity would be used to press the European Union and other nonmembers for counterpart concessions. With successful completion of the Uruguay Round, Asian arguments for "open regionalism," defined as an extension of APEC benefits on an unconditional MFN basis to nonmembers, may be strengthened to avoid undermining the global trade regime. In general, APEC remains an insurance policy for many Asian members, who continue to emphasize a continuation of unilateral liberalization at the national level and further multilateral negotiations in the World Trade Organization (WTO). Equally important, Asian members of APEC have a strong aversion to formal institutions and legally binding obligations: the European Union was used in the EPG reports as a negative model for Asia-Pacific integration. Although the United States, Australia, and Canada are not pressing for rapid institution-building, they are more likely to favor firm and enforceable commitments to negotiated liberalization targets on the model of conventional free trade agreements.

Underlying these different conceptions of APEC's future course are differences between the Asia-Pacific region and either Latin America or Europe. As in the case of European integration, big business has become a vocal lobby in favor of a liberalization agenda in the Pacific. The Pacific Business Forum has been awarded an enhanced role within APEC, and its proposals before the summit were far more ambitious than those of the EPG. Despite the rapid growth of intraregional investment, however, investment links among Pacific economies (and particularly between the United States and East Asia) are smaller in scale than transatlantic ones. As a result, until recently the new agenda of behind-the-border issues—harmonization of domestic practices that restrict access to national markets—has received less attention from members (other than the United States). The traditional GATT agenda of trade liberalization still appears most important for many of the region's political leaders, who are wary of any encroachment on national sovereignty. In addition, American economic leverage, an important element in moving the APEC agenda this far, will decline over the period of APEC liberalization as intra-Asian trade and investment grows more rapidly than trans-Pacific. As the importance of the American market declines relative to intra-Asian trade, an important lever for furthering formal commitments to liberalization will fade as well. Under those circumstances, the less ambitious Asian view of APEC is more likely to dominate.

The New Regionalism, the United States, and Europe

Like European arguments for future regional integration, American rationales for its strategies to sustain integration in the Pacific or the Western Hemisphere have been directed at domestic and regional audiences. U.S. administrations describe the benefits to members and to the United States and discount any costs to nonmembers or the global economic order. Most U.S. analysts have asserted that these regional projects will remain building blocks of the global trade order rather than alternatives to that order. In this optimistic view the United States is most likely to pursue a pragmatic regionalism that will remain coupled with its more traditional strategies of bilateral bargaining and multilateral liberalization in the WTO. Nor is it likely that these regional schemes will be captured very easily by protectionists, although politically powerful sectors did receive favorable terms in NAFTA. International anxieties about NAFTA's implications were allayed by the political cleavages that emerged during the debate over its passage: economic nationalists and protectionists clearly opposed NAFTA, and liberals supported it. This political lineup was very different from the coalitions for and against preferential trading arrangements a half century ago.

To the degree that nonmembers have been engaged, only economic effects in the narrowest sense have been assessed. Asian countries voiced concern over the discriminatory implications of American regional initiatives in North America, but those anxieties have declined since NAFTA has taken effect and its implications have been scrutinized more carefully. The trade diversion effects of NAFTA or a prospective Western Hemispheric FTA are likely to be small and concentrated in particular sectors (textiles and automobiles, for example). Investment diversion effects may be somewhat larger, but they do not leave competitors without recourse: investment climates elsewhere can be made more attractive through policy reforms.[25]

The European Union, the most prominent outsider, has offered few objections so far to these regional initiatives, but it has made clear that it expects "open regionalism" and that it will not be shut out of rapidly growing developing country markets in which it already has substantial stakes. The Commission of the European Union supported completion of NAFTA and found that its trade creation effects were likely to offset any negative economic consequences. The Community did take issue with the discriminatory treatment afforded outsiders in financial services, insurance, and investment, however. The enthusiasm of the United States for APEC and the Pacific during 1993 produced more European anxiety that American attention to the Pacific "would be to the detriment of the Community." The Community also was concerned that APEC was establishing high and exclusionary hurdles to participation in APEC working groups by nonmembers such as the European Community.[26] A more concrete move to counter the effects of American-led regionalism was announced before the Miami Summit of the Americas: plans to negotiate a free trade agreement between the European Union and MERCOSUR. That initiative suggests a competition in liberalization predicted by proponents of the new regionalism.

Narrowly defined economic effects on outsiders often are difficult to estimate before regional agreements are in place. Forecasts of broader effects on the foreign economic policies of the United States and on transatlantic economic relations are even more uncertain. There are few analogies from the American past or contemporary international relations to serve as a guide. European integration is not comparable, since neither Pacific nor Western Hemispheric integration soon will entail institutional elaboration or pooling of sovereignty. Both the Pacific and Latin America include rapidly growing developing countries that remain suspicious of asymmetric relations with a much larger industrialized partner. The United States, particularly Congress, is wary of commitments and institutions that might impinge on its ability to wield trade instruments unilaterally. Liberalization in both regions is likely to be multispeed and to progress relatively slowly. Partly at the prodding of the United States, the regional agendas are ambitious, including issues of domestic regulation that are more complex than conventional trade liberalization.

Despite the benign view that prevails in the United States about these incipient regional commitments, they may have three additional effects that raise concerns about U.S. policy in a regionalized world economy: the consumption of scarce bureaucratic and governmental resources, the use of regional preferential arrangements as bargaining chips, and a growing tendency toward "backyardism" as foreign policy is regionalized.

U.S. policy has never been so deeply involved in significant regional economic enterprises of this kind. Globalists argue—pointing to the European Community—that regional projects will attract a growing share of the political attention and bureaucratic investment that otherwise would be devoted to the global trade regime and to other trading partners, such as Europe. This possibility should be of particular concern when resources for new policy investments of any kind are in short supply in the U.S. government. The trade and foreign affairs bureaucracy in the government is not large; budgetary stringency and ideological opposition are unlikely to permit substantial growth. A decline in real resources is more likely. Adding responsibility for new regional negotiations that may last for years could soon complicate management of the new dispute settlement mechanism at the WTO and reduce the attention devoted to developing a new WTO agenda. The foundations for a more inward-looking and regionally directed foreign economic policy could soon be in place. This turn to regional commitments is even more likely if the WTO disappoints as a forum for negotiation or as a means of resolving trade conflicts, a possibility that is considered later.

Regional projects also could tempt the United States toward economic activism of a new kind: using Western Hemisphere and Asia-Pacific regional arrangements as bargaining chips with the European Union. Rather than turning inward and concentrating on its novel regional roles, the United States could mobilize its regional partners and use the threat of a regional option in order to force concessions from Europe in bilateral or global negotiations. The United States employed this strategy explicitly at the APEC summit in 1993 in order to conclude the Uruguay Round negotiations on more favorable terms. The summit was preoccupied with the design of a common APEC position toward the GATT negotiations. A key role of APEC since its inception has been to lobby within the global trading system for multilateral negotiations and multilateral resolution of outstanding trade conflicts.

C. Fred Bergsten and C. Randall Henning have foreseen an extension of this policy of "ratcheting up" trade liberalization from the regional to the global level during the medium term, when Europe is likely to be particularly absorbed in its internal programs of deepening and widening the EU.[27] Playing the regional card is particularly important vis-à-vis Europe, since the European Union has constructed a web of bilateral and regional preferences on its periphery that award it even greater weight in the international trade regime. Benign rounds of competitive liberalization may not be the dominant outcome, however. A strategy of reciprocal regional bargaining assumes that the United States can "deliver" credibly on liberalization commitments within any Western Hemispheric or Pacific arrangement and then manage the bargaining with Europe on behalf of its regional partners. Such a scenario also assumes considerable skills in diplomatic coordination and intraregional consensus-building. The record of a much more highly institutionalized European Community in this regard is not entirely encouraging.

In a less perfect world, American efforts to extract concessions from Europe on the basis of its regional roles in the Pacific or the Western Hemisphere could lead to discontent on the part of its regional partners and bluff-calling by the Europeans. Rather than competitive liberalization, a hardening of regional arrangements could result.[28] This strategy is not a long step from an orientation in which regional groups bargain directly with one another outside global rules, a longstanding fear of supporters of the WTO and the multilateral trade regime. Awarding a central role to bargaining between regions and quasi-regions could alter the international economic landscape permanently.

Finally, two recent episodes of international bargaining suggest that regionalizing trade and economic policies may create new lines of foreign policy conflict between the United States and the European Union by creating assumptions of regional constituencies and backyards. The selection of a new head for the WTO created fissures that were purely regional in character. Renato Ruggiero, the EU candidate who was chosen eventually, was opposed by candidates from the Western Hemisphere (former President Carlos Salinas of Mexico, backed by the United States) and Asia. As Salinas's chances faded following the Mexican financial crisis, the United States continued to oppose Ruggiero, creating exasperation among EU members. The episode illustrated the emergence of regional constituencies around the United States and the EU. It also suggested a pressing need for new procedures to assign leadership in global economic institutions.

European attitudes during the Mexican financial crisis in January 1995 also demonstrated the power of regional assumptions outside the realm of trade. The U.S. government was criticized for its unilateralism in reaching key decisions, particularly its pressure within the International Monetary Fund for a program of extraordinary size to support Mexico.

Part of the resistance by Britain and Germany, however, de-
rived from their definition of the Mexican crisis as regional
rather than global. Europe did not present a united front;
France was more sympathetic to U.S. arguments. Nevertheless, IMF executive directors from Switzerland, the Nether-
lands, and Norway joined Germany and Britain in abstaining
on the Mexican program.[29] Whether the systemic effects of
the Mexican crisis would have been catastrophic without the
package devised by the U.S. administration remains a controversial question. Choosing to define particular issues as
global and others as regional responsibilities during a crisis,
however, is an indicator of the longer-term effects that regionalization may have. Of course, delimiting regional
spheres is a time-honored diplomatic practice. In this case,
such regional backyards were used to disclaim responsibility
rather than to claim prerogatives of action.

EUROPEAN INSTITUTIONAL EVOLUTION
AND RELATIONS WITH THE UNITED STATES

The European Union and its members confront a new American enthusiasm for regional projects of which Europe is not
a part. The United States has accepted regionalism in Europe
since the formation of the European Community. Although
American support for European integration was a constant of
the Cold War years, that support mingled with concern over
the economic costs that integration might impose on the
United States. The end of the Cold War might be expected to
force the United States to a skeptical recalculation of the
costs and benefits of European integration. Initiatives to establish a single European market and support for European
Union stabilization and integration in central and eastern Europe have sustained American consensus on the value of European integration, however. Some Atlanticists appear even

more supportive of a federal European future than European public opinion.[30]

Although they accept the benefits of deepening and widening the European Union, some observers have become more skeptical, not of the strictly economic benefits or costs of European integration but of the inward-looking stance and cumbersome decision-making of the EU. A recent study of conflict between the United States and the European Community over the liberalization of financial services notes that the Community paid little attention to the external implications of its 1992 program until the United States complained about particular aspects of the Commission's plans.[31] More broadly, the inflexible negotiating style and reactive policy stance of the EC in trade diplomacy has been criticized.[32] A recent report on U.S.–European Community relations compared negotiating with the EC to "shaking hands with a multiheaded octopus, so diffuse and contradictory are its methods of dealing with international partners."[33] Despite this disquiet regarding the institutional form rather than the fact of European integration, U.S. intervention in debates over European institution-building has been relatively rare and seldom timely enough to influence the process. And despite the importance of the Economic and Monetary Union for the United States and for the international monetary system, the U.S. Treasury remained virtually silent as the plans for EMU were debated in Europe.[34]

Scholars have provided relatively little assistance to policymakers in assessing the external implications of European institutional choices. Clear relationships between national political institutions and patterns of foreign policy have been difficult to establish. The European Union, assigning important roles to both national governments and European institutions in a dense negotiating network, is a far more complicated object of study. External analysts have been most concerned with the balance between Community institutions and national governments in European decision-making, a question that reflects on core theoretical debates in international relations. Few assessments have been made of the consequences for outsiders of the institutional balance that is struck and the form that it takes.

The reluctance of both scholars and policymakers to assess the external consequences of European integration reflects the broad constituency that the European Community has maintained on both sides of the Atlantic: a predisposition toward an entity that has overcome ancient nationalist enmities and represents a "strong" form of international cooperation. Given past American paternalism, observers and policymakers in the United States have been hesitant to comment on the internal evolution of European integration. Europeans often have responded to such attention with a prickly resistance to what is seen as oversight by their Atlantic partner. Nevertheless, theorists of cooperation have long recognized that cooperative bargains within one group may disadvantage those who are not members (a finding mirrored in the theory of preferential trading areas). The Common Agricultural Policy (CAP) is a classic example of highly institutionalized cooperation—a policy area in which the EC approaches a federal structure—that has imposed significant costs on nonmembers.

Failure to take into account the external effects of regional institution-building only confirms the inward-looking character of regional enterprises. The European Union is poised to debate and decide on its next institutional steps in preparation for the 1996 intergovernmental conference (IGC). Other regional groups are making initial decisions about institutional design. This may be an opportune moment to scrutinize more carefully the effects that particular institutional paths could have on Europe's external stance and its relations with the United States.

What are the desirable characteristics of regional institutions from the point of view of nonmembers? Three seem particularly important. First, decision-making should be transparent: nonmembers should know where decisions are made within the institutions and by whom. Nonmembers also should be able to track the process of decision-making over time.[35] Second, the regional entity—if it has a delegated external role—should be able to make, change, and implement credible bargains. This criterion of judgment—which has been the source of most criticisms of the EC—in turn implies clarity of *competence*, ability to *coordinate* internally, and reasonable *efficiency* in reaching a common position. If the competence of regional institutions vis-à-vis their members is blurred, nonmembers will have great difficulty in bargaining with the regional entity. An effective means of coordinating member governments as well as regional institutions implies the ability to reach a common position, to change that position if necessary in the course of negotiation, and to indicate the means of implementation of any bargain reached. Decision-making efficiency denotes internal processes that have an end point and avoid a pattern of cycling.

Each of these criteria for assessing a regional arrangement also should be acceptable to the members of that group. A more controversial criterion—and one that reflects directly on the economic benefits and costs of a preferential regional arrangement—is that institutions should not systematically bias decisions in favor of rent-seeking or protectionist coalitions. Obviously, such interests within a region will mobilize to capture its regional institutions for their own gain. Those competing with such interests outside the region will not want an institutional design that makes the task of capture easier.

Predicting the institutional evolution of the European Union is particularly difficult at this time. The usual cycles of Euro-phoria and Euro-pessimism have become even more compressed in the 1990s; the peaks and troughs seem more pronounced. After the success of the single-market initiative and the negotiation of the Maastricht Treaty, the European project seemed to reach a premature dead end with the Danish and French referenda and the 1992–93 monetary crises, which seemed to derail the Maastricht blueprint for Economic and Monetary Union. Since then pessimism has lifted somewhat: planning for EMU proceeds and enlargement to the east is no longer defined as a distant goal.

Uncertainties remain. Even the institutional results of the Maastricht Treaty are subject to competing interpretations. Some label Maastricht a sign that "European affairs will be more deeply influenced by the interests and needs of the nation-states comprising the Union than by the authorities in Brussels"; others view it as "another milestone in the long and complex process of incremental integration in Europe."[36] The 1996 IGC appears more likely to "fine tune" the Maastricht Treaty than to engage in another wave of European institution-building.[37] Whatever the precise rate or shape of future institutional evolution, however, the post-Maastricht debate already has illuminated several issues that will remain on the agenda of the European Union and will affect its external policy. Those issues are the shape of Economic and Monetary Union, the most detailed plan for integration in the Maastricht Treaty; dealing with the "democratic deficit"; the implications of subsidiarity; and the architecture and consequences of enlargement to a Europe of 15 members and more.

Economic and monetary union: divided competence and policy coordination. The Maastricht Treaty contains a detailed timetable for achieving Economic and Monetary Union in three stages. Apart from the stipulated timetable, the shape of EMU closely matched the desires of European central banks and particularly the German central bank: strict economic convergence criteria as necessary prerequisites for monetary union and a European central bank dedicated to price stability and independent of political influence.[38] Less than a year after the treaty was signed, the European Monetary System was undermined by successive currency crises induced by Germany's response to the economic shock of reunification. Whether a fixed exchange rate system in Europe with free capital mobility and national monetary policies was inherently unstable remained a disputed point. The exchange rate crises of 1992–93 and the widening of fluctuation margins in the Exchange Rate Mechanism (ERM) appeared to set back the timetable for EMU. Although a recent European Commission green paper does not rule out the possibility of instituting EMU in 1997, most observers and national governments now seem to aim at 1999. The introduction of a common currency for the European public would occur after EMU in the early years of the next century.[39]

Arguments over the appropriate path to EMU and its timing have obscured some of the issues raised by its institutional design for global economic management. The institutions of EMU appear highly centralized: the model of a national monetary authority is transposed to the European level, permitting the Commission to emphasize the advantages of "Europe speaking with one voice" in international monetary affairs. Viewed from the outside, however, the proposed structure raises questions of competence and coordination that could thwart more ambitious proposals for macroeconomic coordination in the Group of Seven (G-7) leading industrialized nations.

The European System of Central Banks and the European Central Bank that will be established before the beginning of Phase Three of EMU are designed for political independence: terms on the Executive Board of the ECB are nonrenewable; the only shareholders are national central banks. In one key respect, the autonomy of the ECB may be greater than that of some national central banks, since the oversight of the European Parliament is arguably weaker than that of certain national legislatures. The role of the ECB in setting European monetary policy will be supreme, and the goal set—price stability—is simple and unique. Its influence over other economic policy instruments is more limited. In managing the exchange rate of the European currency, the Council of Ministers shares responsibility with the ECB (Article 109 of the Maastricht Treaty). The Council's aims in managing the exchange rate may not be dominated by a concern for price stability, however, and a potential for conflict lies in these differing policy orientations. The ECB is obliged to intervene in foreign exchange markets in support of the Council's policies, but it is not required to use monetary policy.[40] As Peter Kenen suggests, if managing the exchange rate or coordinating its management with others has negative implications for price stability (as it might if large-scale intervention were attempted), the new European monetary authorities might attempt to earn credibility by resisting such collaboration.[41]

The meshing of internal and external coordination is further complicated by the continuing role of national finance ministries in setting fiscal policy. Since one criticism that has been leveled at recent G-7 policy coordination is an over-reliance on monetary policy, this national hold on fiscal instruments makes improvements in international coordination more difficult. Rather than the simplified vision of Europe "speaking with one voice," in a Group of Three, what appears more likely is an even more complex G-7 process in which "the chain of command and relative responsibility are almost certain to become more muddled."[42] Henning argues that the Maastricht Treaty's requirement of unanimity in the Council before any agreement can be instituted means that future efforts to stabilize exchange rates in industrialized countries will be difficult—EMU institutional design is biased in favor of exchange rate flexibility.[43] Others' prognosis is even more pessimistic: internal coordination problems will render any European participation in international monetary coordination less credible—if such participation would occur, which is not clear. By reducing European vulnerability to the vagaries of American policy, economic and monetary union would lower European interest in global policy coordination. Institutional obstacles could reinforce that structural turn away from international monetary collaboration.

These institutional barriers to participation by the EU in future G-7 policy coordination could be seen as no more serious than those confronted by national governments that deal with independent central banks. On the other hand, as Kenen suggests, the EMU could be an example of the way in which a centralized and highly institutionalized form of European cooperation produces "more exchange rate instability in the world at large."[44]

The democratic deficit. Three democratic deficits have been identified in the European Union. When measured against their populations, existing voting formulas in the Council of Ministers overrepresent its smaller members. Revising those formulas has proven to be a very contentious issue. A second definition of the democratic deficit assigns it to the relatively weak powers of the European Parliament. Finally, national parliaments could be awarded a greater role within the European Union.[45]

Germany has pressed for the second, federalist remedy to the deficit: expanding the role of the European Parliament. Both the Single European Act and the Maastricht Treaty expanded the legislative powers of the Parliament (although in the important areas of agriculture and trade, the Parliament is only consulted by other Community institutions, as in the past). Maastricht also involved the legislature more deeply in the confirmation of the Commission and its president. After the designation of Jacques Santer as Commission president, the Parliament wielded its new right to be "consulted," awarding the new president a narrow vote of confirmation in July 1994.

The powers of the European Parliament may be further expanded following the 1996 IGC. Would this reduction of the democratic deficit be in the interests of nonmembers? Glancing at the role of the U.S. Congress, one might argue that democratized European decision-making will only provide better access for protectionist and antiliberal forces, forces that are more effectively restrained under the current institutions. It is doubtful that such interests would find a more congenial home in the European Parliament, whose members are elected in relatively large constituencies on the basis of proportional representation, than they have found in the Community's current institutional configuration. Recent interventions by the Parliament on issues related to internal liberalization and the single market do not suggest an antiliberal policy bias.[46]

Reducing the democratic deficit through the award of greater powers to the European Parliament also might produce institutional benefits from the point of view of the United States and other nonmembers. A more powerful European Parliament could increase the transparency of EU decision-making: among the changes agreed in the Maastricht Treaty was an increase in the Parliament's oversight and investigatory powers. Skeptics argue, however, that the gradual increase in parliamentary powers has increased the complexity of EU decision-making when viewed from the outside.[47] Evidence from legislative experience since the Single European Act also suggests that greater parliamentary involvement need not diminish decision-making efficiency in the EU. Parliamentary powers could serve to make agreements completed by the EU more credible.[48] If adequate powers are delegated to the Commission, that increase in credibility could be purchased without reducing the EU's negotiating flexibility.

Enlarging the influence of national parliaments is seldom offered as an answer to the EU's democratic deficit. If the European Parliament cannot be accused of catering to particularistic interests, national parliaments often are. In this view, internal liberalization is owed to European Community technocrats and national executives.[49] The current institutional balance, which helps to insulate national executives, also enables them to undertake politically controversial policies of liberalization. Those policies might be impossible if affected interests are provided with a greater legislative role through which they could obstruct and delay. Lisa Martin has countered that national parliaments necessarily will play a role in European policymaking for the foreseeable future. Rather than serving as a barrier to further integration and home to protectionist interests, the early involvement of national parliaments in European issues produces a higher rate of implementation of EU directives.[50] The role of national parliaments in creating and maintaining a single European policy space is a benefit to those with an interest in European integration, including U.S. exporters and investors.

Leaving aside the unpredictable and all-important question of which political forces will dominate the European and national parliaments of the future and what their policy preferences will be, democratization of the EU appears to have positive implications for the economic and foreign policy interests of nonmembers.

Subsidiarity. The appropriate allocation of responsibility for policies among the European, national, regional, and local levels became part of the debate over the future of European institutions when it was included explicitly in the Maastricht Treaty. The history of the concept explains its ill-defined character. Subsidiarity was originally used by Christian Democrats to justify an enlargement of the role of Community institutions. By the time of the Maastricht conference, it had become a means for the critics of a federal Europe—whether

British Conservatives or German *Länder*—to restrain what were perceived as encroachments on their competence by an overcentralized Community.[51] At Maastricht the term was acceptable to interests with widely different views of the European future, in large measure because it was empty of clear content. The working principles of subsidiarity have been "surprisingly unclear and informal, and they do not appear to rest upon a compelling economic or legal logic."[52] The implications of subsidiarity therefore will depend on future interpretation and application as the European Union evolves.

If, as the post-Maastricht period suggests, subsidiarity leads toward greater decentralization—an emphasis on accountability rather than on the centralized coordination of national policies—then the effects on EU nonmembers, such as the United States, could be mixed. If decentralization entails an erosion of the single market that gradually has been created in Europe, one of the greatest benefits offered by the EU to nonmembers would be undermined. Of course, the decentralization of certain policies would have little impact on economic transactions. Some interpretations of subsidiarity would place European policies with negative consequences for outsiders back at the national level (although that movement is unlikely outside the realm of theory).[53] The transfer of regulatory policies to the national or subnational (regional) level from the European, however, could increase transaction costs significantly and create disguised barriers to investment and trade. Although discussions of subsidiarity often assume that accountability increases as the scale of government declines, confusion of competences could reduce the transparency of policymaking as well. Depending on its definition in particular policy realms, the implementation of subsidiarity, that portmanteau concept of the post-Maastricht era, could have significant effects on the interests of nonmembers.

Enlargement (widening). Perhaps the most widely discussed feature of the EU's future evolution is the inclusion of new members and its consequences for European institutions. The United States strongly supports enlargement of the European Union to central and eastern Europe; the beneficial foreign policy effects of enlargement remain an important rationale for American support of European integration. If the EU's role in stabilizing its eastern neighbors faltered or if EU policies toward them veered in an unhelpful direction (of which there is no sign), American attitudes toward the EU might change significantly.

Apart from U.S. concern with the success of widening the European Union, two distinct effects could flow from enlargement and affect the interests of nonmembers. First, new members might change the balance of preferences within the EU over a range of policies, given their different economic endowments, foreign policy interests, or political ideologies. Enlargement of the EU to 15 members in 1995 with the accession of Austria, Finland, and Sweden may tilt its policies in particular directions. The newest members probably will join the more liberal (in economic terms) "northern" tier of the EU, pressing for policies that are less protectionist and less sympathetic to state subsidies for uncompetitive industries. On the other hand, these members protect their agricultural sectors even more heavily than the EU. Their membership in the CAP will reduce some of the pressure to extend its reforms by providing a market for the agricultural products of existing EU members. Domestic politics probably will make them eager proponents of the Social Charter and protection for labor in the EU. They will enhance the activism of the EU in eastern Europe through their own security concerns with the region and their comfortable budgets. Weighing against this foreign policy activism is their history as neutrals, which may make them skeptical of a common foreign and security policy, particularly its defense dimension. Institutionally, the three new members, or at least the Nordic two, are likely to favor subsidiarity (defined as opposition to further centralization).[54]

The policy preferences of future EU members from central and eastern Europe are more difficult to predict, since membership may be years away. If the record of Mediterranean members is any guide, these members would reinforce the coalition of the "poor" favoring increased structural spending and press for a shift of CAP resources in their direction. Unlike earlier members, they are likely to favor EU development of a common defense, given their security concerns. If the 1995 members tilt in the other direction on defense issues, then the east European agenda could increase conflict over the evolution of a common EU security policy.[55]

The institutional effects of enlargement are even more difficult to predict, since the EU has used enlargement in the past to expedite institutional reform. Institutional debate centers on the effects of enlargement on the efficiency of Community decision-making. If a streamlined decision-making system is not introduced following the 1996 IGC, further enlargement could paralyze the EU. The Single European Act introduced greater reliance on qualified majority voting (as opposed to unanimity) to expedite the single-market initiatives and to "transform (albeit selectively) decision-making within the Council of Ministers."[56] The particular formula chosen for a qualified majority (54 out of 76 votes) also served to prevent some predictable and persistent coalitions from forming: the new regime became one of shifting coalitions.[57]

Future changes could include enhanced use of qualified majority voting, changing the formulas for qualified majorities (the point of contention in the European Free Trade Association accession), or reordering the voting weights of individual states. Possible representation formulas also are possible; in some proposals, smaller members would form constituencies similar to those in the IMF. A similar problem of streamlining arises for the Commission, which is rapidly approaching an unwieldy size. Strenuous objections by the United Kingdom during negotiations for the accession of the EFTA members—countries that closely resembled the existing membership—suggest that such adjustments in internal decision rules and national representation will be very difficult to negotiate. Not only are the United Kingdom and other antifederalist members resistant to the extension of the qualified majority voting, overrepresented smaller members will defend their prerogatives as well.

Any increase in decision-making efficiency that reduces the power of a single member or a small group of members to obstruct EU decision-making is likely to be welcomed by the United States and other outsiders. Of course, a requirement of unanimity can be used by economic liberals as well as those attempting to protect threatened national industries or slow external opening. Nevertheless, a decision-making system that avoids the "joint-decision trap" is more likely to give up old policies that have been captured by vested interests and to respond in an innovative way to changed external conditions.[58] Such decision-making streamlining also is likely to provide external negotiating partners with a more flexible and credible interlocutor.

Enlargement also implies more heterogeneous preferences and characteristics among members, which may not be dealt with as readily through institutional fixes of the type just described. One solution agreed at Maastricht is even more politically charged than proposals to enhance efficiency in EU decision-making: the creation of a multispeed Europe or a Europe of "variable geometry." Both the United Kingdom and Denmark were granted opt-out protocols that they could employ before stage three of EMU; the United Kingdom also was allowed to opt out of the social protocol accepted by the other eleven members.[59] This partial fragmentation of the EU edifice for existing members is likely to be replicated in the accession of prospective members from central and eastern Europe. These poorer and more agricultural countries also pose a threat to the institutional influence of smaller states in the EU: many predict a lengthy transition before full membership.[60] In the meantime, the thicket of association agreements in central and eastern Europe threatens to become "an organizational labyrinth" rather than a new "European architecture."[61] Avoiding this complex hub-and-spoke arrangement with its lack of transparency and high transaction costs would require the design of a series of "halfway houses" or "waiting rooms" that would incorporate these countries into a European framework without either moving rapidly to full membership or constructing a less-than-full-membership category.

A Europe of variable geometry may imply different concessions to heterogeneity that have different implications for institutional development in the European Union and for the economic interests of nonmembers such as the United States. "Multispeed" implies a common destination but different timing in reaching it, timing that is dependent on particular characteristics of each country (such as level of income). Such transitional arrangements are familiar from other international institutions, but differentiation in institutional obligations is assumed to be temporary. A common set of institutions and commitments remains for all "full" members. What appeared at Maastricht was Europe à la carte— Denmark and the United Kingdom might not share a common destination with the other members of the EU. Using this model, the European Union would become a linked alliance of several "communities of the like-minded" defined by their different policy commitments (for example, a Europe of EMU).

This type of differentiation, if adopted and extended, could impose substantial costs on those trading and investing in the European Union and in its prospective members. The predictability and credibility of the unified European policy regime would be eroded in favor of a patchwork that would increase transaction costs for those outside the EU. For external interlocutors, the issue of competence and representation would loom large. Who speaks for Europe in a particular policy space might become a question. The means of governance in such a variegated Europe have not been addressed: a complex series of institutions would be required for different issue areas, reducing transparency in decision-making.

European debates on the effects of widening and the institutional boundaries of deepening have only begun. The recent presentation of a report by the German Christian Democrats that urged a multispeed Europe and nominated a particular "hard core" of existing members to forge ahead toward economic and political union created a storm of negative reactions from the "soft fringe." A completely unified policy regime for Europe—both prospective and current EU members—has disappeared, at least temporarily. Whether the fragmentation ends with the United Kingdom and Denmark or touches other members, the particular shape chosen for a multispeed Europe and the permanence awarded to that institutional architecture will impinge on the interests of those standing outside the EU.

None of these institutional dilemmas is unique to the European Union. NAFTA and the Western Hemisphere face similar choices in widening regional agreements. The institutional choices of the European Union have much greater import, however, given the EU's highly developed cooperative structure and its weight in the international economy. Even this survey suggests how difficult it is to calculate the effects of institutional alternatives on the EU as an international actor. Nevertheless, the EU's institutional choices should take into account the interests of nonmembers. External scrutiny is not illegitimate, nor need it thwart further integration: the forces that will drive or obstruct European integration are largely internal. The United States will continue to favor European economic integration, but it should calculate more carefully the consequences of specific institutional responses to European integration for its own economic and foreign policy interests. Its reading of institutional consequences should be voiced earlier rather than later in debates on Europe's institutional future. At the same time, the United States and other nonmembers must temper their concerns with an acknowledgment that institutional innovations in Europe are rooted in intricate internal bargains forged through extended negotiation. Those who are not members should be heard, but their influence will be limited.

TRANSATLANTIC ECONOMIC CONFLICT AND SYSTEM FRICTION

Perhaps the most pessimistic reading of the effects of regionalization on transatlantic relations concerns the underlying sources of economic conflict between Europe and the United States. Rather than simple protectionism, conflict increasingly might center on "unfair competition" and "level playing fields"—terms defined less by any measurable barriers to market access than by presumed differences between two distinct capitalist political economies. (If one adds Japan, then the clash of systems involves at least three distinct models.) The European Union, in this view, represents more than a collection of coordinated policies or even a set of distinct institutions: it incorporates a distinctive social and economic order, in contradistinction to "North America." Michael Smith and Stephen Woolcock argue, for example, that the end of the Cold War has revealed fundamental "systemic" and "structural" differences between the United States and Europe that make transatlantic relations more difficult to manage.[62] Stanley Hoffmann notes that many Europeans, particularly those devoted to European integration, see the vocation of the European Community as "the defense of West European distinctiveness, the preservation of those features of West European societies which, despite 'Americanization' (industrialization in a capitalist framework) still distinguished them from America's society and polity."[63] If transatlantic economic conflicts represent deeper fault lines between different capitalist political economies, the final battles of the Uruguay Round—over agriculture and the audiovisual sector—were not simple trade conflicts but one episode in a long-running and possibly deepening rift between the United States and Europe.

The expansion of the "trade" agenda from barriers to access at the border to a wide range of behind-the-border policies has been part of U.S. commercial policy at the global and regional levels. The agenda is even longer and more diffuse in American relations with Japan and other East Asian societies than it is vis-à-vis the European Union. Issues of harmonization and mutual recognition of national policies also have been part of the intra-European agenda. As described earlier, this expansion in the agenda of international economic relations is one motivation for the construction of regional arrangements, in which small numbers and (perhaps) greater similarities in domestic systems may permit easier resolution of such conflicts.

Three trends have encouraged the turn toward this more extensive agenda: growing links between trade and investment; the elaboration of strategic trade theory; and the implications of "new" regulation (labor standards, environment, consumer health and safety) for trade policy. The importance of investment in setting this new agenda was described earlier. Barriers to and manipulation of investment increasingly are seen as significant impediments to the expansion of exports and instruments for altering national competitive advantage. The more ambitious implications of strategic trade theory have been disavowed by many of its scholarly proponents; nevertheless, that theoretical turn directed attention to behind-the-border policies that could alter the advantages of national firms in particular sectors. (Whether new trade theory pointed to greater government intervention in response is disputed.) Finally, and perhaps of greatest political significance, new agenda items have appeared through political means: groups that advocate greater regulation in the interests of higher labor standards, environmental protection, or consumer health and safety have urged international action to restrain competitive pressures that might undermine national regulatory policies. The "level playing field" has, through such political intervention, been defined to include an ever wider span of social policies.[64] At the same time, exporters and investors have challenged such regulatory differences as sometime impediments to market access that should be targeted in international negotiations.

"System friction" is a phrase coined by Sylvia Ostry to describe conflicts of this new variety. System friction differs from old-style trade conflict in two important respects, and both suggest that economic conflicts of the new type will be more intractable than the old. First, the question of what should be on the "trade" (or economic) agenda is itself a point of controversy: the criteria for inclusion often are vaguely stated competitive effects. Since many of the policies or practices (they need not be government policies) are deeply entrenched in domestic interests, resistance to international scrutiny of these "domestic" policies is intense.[65] Second, issues in systemic conflicts are believed to be linked in a way that sectoral trade negotiations are not. The policies or practices in question are part of a politico-economic system that cannot be disentangled readily—changing one policy may risk an unraveling of another (or risk political opposition from its supporters). Suzanne Berger and Ronald

Dore have labeled this quality "tightness of fit": "institutions do not stand alone but depend for their good functioning on inputs that other parts of the system provide."[66]

Two features of the U.S.–European economic relationship should be emphasized before examining evidence of transatlantic system friction. First, if these regional systems are experiencing a great deal of conflict, it has not prevented one of the highest levels of economic interconnection in the world economy. The data are clear. The EU and the United States are the world's largest trading partners: their bilateral trade in 1993 constituted seven percent of total world trade. Transatlantic investment links are even more striking (once again in contrast to Japan). On a stock basis, EU firms contributed more than half of all foreign direct investment in the United States; U.S. investment in the EU represents about 40 percent of the total American stock of foreign investment.[67]

Second, to portray either of the two regions—North America or the European Union—as coherent politico-economic systems is difficult, since the heterogeneity within each region is so marked. Attitudes toward social welfare expenditures and industrial subsidies in Canada are closer to European models than to those in the United States. Since 1979, Britain under Conservative governments often has been joined to the United States in an "Anglo-American" model of market-based capitalism that is distinguished from a continental European or "Rhineland" model epitomized by Germany. (That there is an "Asian" model of capitalism based on Japan is even more dubious.) Despite these deviations around regional means, the contrasts between the United States and the European Union on a range of economic policies is great enough to take the system friction argument seriously.

The best starting point for an examination of transatlantic economic friction is the complaints of trade malfeasance made by the European Union and the United States against each other. Their annual reports on barriers to trade and investment, taken together, give a reasonably accurate portrait of the issues that loom largest on their bilateral agenda.[68] The pattern that emerges from these sources is clear: U.S. complaints concern European policies of "unfair" or protective public support for particular sectors; European complaints are strongest regarding American "aggressive unilateralism" in commercial diplomacy that is directed at precisely these practices. A superficial case for system friction appears to exist. Only closer examination of a selection of these issues—American unilateralism; European policies toward agriculture, the audio-visual sector, and subsidies to industry; and the new agenda items of labor standards and the environment—can demonstrate whether the pattern of conflict is genuinely systemic and whether means exist to resolve these conflicts.

"Aggressive Unilateralism" in American Trade Policy

The particular circumstances of American economic policy in the early 1980s were described earlier. In addition to a shift toward regional and bilateral preferential arrangements, the number of actions brought against "unfair" trading practices—antidumping, countervailing duties (subsidies), and Section 301—increased dramatically: "no other economic regulatory program took on such an increase in caseloads."[69] In part this reflected the competitive pressures induced by the overvalued dollar (although the cases remained on a relatively high plateau even after the dollar declined), in part the growing importance of behind-the-border policies and changing definitions of "unfairness," and in part redesign of trade policy rules to increase access for affected firms. For trading partners of the United States, the most objectionable American policies were those labeled "aggressive unilateralism" by Jagdish Bhagwati ("super" and "special" 301) in which the United States determined that trade was unfair (whether GATT obligations had been violated or not) and then demanded "market opening" measures from targeted trading partners under threat of American retaliation.[70]

The European Union was not a primary target of Section 301 measures, and its share of these actions has declined over time. The cases brought against the EU were overwhelmingly—19 out of 22.5—directed at the Common Agricultural Policy (to be discussed later).[71] Nevertheless, these and other (antidumping and countervailing duties) actions brought against the European Union were major transatlantic irritants. The EU also has objected to U.S. unilateralism in extending its jurisdictional reach over non-American corporations located outside the United States. Here the list of actions was long and often was related to environmental issues (the Marine Mammals Protection Act) or foreign policy goals (export controls and trade sanctions imposed on Cuba).

The EU is not alone in objecting to these American trade practices. Recent international criticism of threatened U.S. trade sanctions against the Japanese automobile industry demonstrate that the European Union is not alone in its dislike of American unilateralism. The future of these practices and their effect on transatlantic economic relations depend on several features of the American trade policy environment. The evolution of practices and policies targeted in the European Union, particularly the Common Agricultural Policy, is of central importance. Vis-à-vis the EU, there is little evidence that the use of instruments directed at "unfair" trade has expanded laterally into new issue areas during the 1990s. Equally important is whether the United States will pursue "aggressive multilateralism," as recommended by Thomas O. Bayard and Kimberly Elliott. The new dispute settlement mechanism of the World Trade Organization was designed to meet American specifications in most respects. Many past unilateral actions by the United States would now violate

WTO rules and potentially impose new costs on the country. Although evidence that aggressive unilateralism damaged the GATT system during the 1980s is slender, that risk is higher following the completion of the Uruguay Round. The recent U.S.–Japan trade dispute over the automobile sector appears to demonstrate the limits of U.S. support for multi-lateral dispute settlement: old-style unilateralism has been combined with WTO complaints. Whether the United States and the EU will employ the new WTO as a means of conflict resolution is a central question for their future economic relationship, one considered at greater length later.

The United States also may decide that the prospects for successful deployment of its unilateral trade arsenal have declined in the 1990s. The symmetric character of its trade relations with Europe made success less likely in transatlantic disputes, even in earlier periods; as other trading partners become less dependent on the American market, U.S. pursuit of market opening through unilateral means may decline. Ironically, another form of symmetry also may induce greater American restraint: emulation by its trading partners, who plan their own versions of Section 301, antidumping (the EU is well equipped in this area), and countervailing duties. Sir Leon Brittan has proposed a new EU trade policy measure, labeled the illicit practices regulation, that bears a close resemblance to Section 301. Despite claims that the instrument would be used in support of WTO obligations, the EU has not forsworn its possible use against nonmembers of the WTO or in areas where WTO rules "are lacking or incomplete."[72] In the realm of countervailing duties, the EU also is crafting policies much closer to those of the United States; its freedom of maneuver has been increased by the Uruguay Round agreement on agriculture, since threats of retaliation against European subsidies in that sector, long a restraint on EU action, are now much less likely. EU actions are also more credible since a simple majority in the Council of Ministers is now sufficient for antidumping and countervailing duties actions: liberal trading countries will find blocking such measures much more difficult.[73] Although the new trade policies available to the EU may not be directed against the United States, the possibility of tit-for-tat retaliation is more real than it was in the past.

Government Intervention and Protection in the European Union

U.S. complaints against the European Union center on its view of the appropriate role for government in a capitalist economy, particularly the issue of subsidies for and protection of specific sectors. The United States is not free of such policies, despite its self-image as the home of market capitalism. Europeans point to subsidies provided by individual states and the more or less disguised support provided to technology-intensive sectors by the Defense Department. Nevertheless, the United States has been the *demandeur* in most instances of conflict over state assistance to agriculture and industry.

Agriculture. It is an oddity of contemporary transatlantic conflict that a sector of declining economic importance with a small and shrinking workforce should receive so much attention and produce such high-stakes confrontations. Yet the sun never seems to set on this particular sunset industry. Kym Anderson has proposed one model to explain how such an electorally and economically declining sector could receive large-scale public support in industrialized economies—a level of support that has grown as industrialization has proceeded.[74] That trend casts a pessimistic pall over the future of transatlantic conflict in this sector, as does the record of the Uruguay Round, in which conflict over agriculture threatened to derail the trade talks until the last cliff-hanging episode in

December 1993.[75] European-American conflict over agriculture worsened in the 1980s as European efforts to expand exports of agriculture products collided with a crisis in the U.S. agricultural sector. The decline of American exports to the EC during these years and growing EC competition with American exporters in third markets only exacerbated American hostility toward the Common Agricultural Policy.[76]

Successful completion and ratification of the Uruguay Round results will bring to a close one chapter in agricultural trade conflict. The agreement brought agriculture under a GATT/WTO regimen for the first time, a major aim of the United States.[77] Beyond that accomplishment, evaluations of the accord and its implications for U.S.–EU discord are mixed. Optimists, such as Anderson, argue that the negotiations served as a useful external shock to domestic systems of agricultural support and may have reinforced an eventual downward trend in their levels. In addition, the GATT/WTO agreement restrains the future policies of rapidly industrializing countries from the same path of burgeoning supports. The agreement also has a ratchet effect: it would be difficult to backslide in an overt way without endangering other key parts of the trade agreement. More pessimistic observers view the negotiated changes as incremental at best and see the nine-year "peace clause" (Article 13) as simple legitimation of undesirable policies.[78]

Unless the CAP is reformed fundamentally, the peace clause will be only a longish truce in this war of attrition. In the medium term, two developments may move changes in the CAP beyond the reforms of the early 1990s: budgetary pressure, reinforced by both the convergence criteria of the EMU and the high levels of debt that most EU governments have assumed during the latest recession, and enlargement of the EU in eastern and central Europe. Unlike the three new entrants to the EU, whose agricultural sectors are even more heavily cosseted and uncompetitive than that of the twelve, prospective members of the EU in east and central Europe could become highly competitive agricultural exporters. One of the major obstacles to their early entry into the EU is the effect that their agricultural surpluses would have on the CAP.

Running counter to these trends is the political economy of agriculture in Europe. In all industrialized countries, for reasons detailed by Anderson, the domestic pressures to reduce or eliminate agricultural subsidies are weak; even more than most consumer interests, the demand for cheap food has not inspired a powerful internal constituency that could counter the agricultural lobby. The demonstrated environmental harm inflicted by highly subsidized agriculture might suggest that an increasingly powerful environmental movement would play the opposition role. In Europe, however, a part of the political power of the agricultural lobby is owed to its success in capturing an image of environmental importance and a symbolic role for a particular way of life. In assessing the significance of these strategies and their resonance with wider European publics, one also is assessing whether agriculture is and will remain a core element in system friction between Europe and the United States.

The theme of agriculture as more than another industry was eloquently expressed in the Commission's 1991 report on the CAP: "Sufficient numbers of farmers must be kept on the land. There is no other way to preserve the natural environment, traditional landscapes and a model of agriculture based on the family farm as favored by the society generally."[79] More efficient policies of direct subsidies are rejected by "peasants" who view themselves as sturdy individualists. Anthropologist Susan Carol Rogers describes the ways in which French views of "the peasant" may embody much more politically charged and culturally profound differences between American and French society: farming as key to the general national interest, a more activist view of the state, a central part of historical identity.[80] To the degree that European agriculture continues to possess such wider cultural connections, the case for continuing system friction may seem strong. Nevertheless, such political and cultural attachments can be satisfied in ways that are less damaging to those outside a particular system: by redefining much of agricultural policy as regional or environmental policy, for example, and changing the instruments of sectoral support. Whether the targets of that support—the farmers—will countenance such changes is less certain.

Protecting European culture: the audio-visual sector. Another highly contentious issue at the close of the Uruguay Round, one that was not resolved to American satisfaction, were the EU's policies in the audio-visual (film and broadcasting) sector. Although the United States was able to ensure that this sector was included under the new General Agreement on Trade in Services, the EU refused to make specific commitments to liberalize the sector. In its narrowest terms, the dispute originated in the Commission's 1989 Broadcast Directive, which reserved a majority of broadcast transmission time for programs of European origin "where practicable" and "by appropriate means." In other respects the audio-visual dispute resembles conflict over agriculture. The issue has been portrayed as one with wider implications for European and national identity. European distress at the encroachment of outsiders on their cultural domain has been long-standing: from British distaste for Canadian (rather than Australian) press barons early in this century, to distrust of the first American cultural "invasion" in the 1920s and 1930s.[81] The Commission's design of a European media policy fits this pattern. The putative aim of the directive—establishing a single market in broadcasting—has been less successful, since much broadcasting simply does not travel readily across national borders. The principal obstacle is not

American competition but the continued fragmentation of European linguistic and cultural space.[82]

As in agriculture, definition of the dispute is a central part of the conflict between the European Union and the United States. Does EU policy represent a distinctive European view of television programs and films as "cultural artifacts" in contrast to American treatment of cultural property as "simple commodities"?[83] Or is the issue, as the United States contends, one of simple and blatant protectionism? Whatever the transatlantic resolution of this more profound issue, EU efforts to increase protection of this sector have faced growing political and technological obstacles. The French government pressed in early 1995 for tightening European broadcasting quotas on foreign programming. In a pattern familiar from other trade and industrial policy issues, Germany and Britain opposed any intensification of restrictions; Italy favored the status quo. The Commission itself was divided on the proposal, and there were protests from European industry as well. (Even the earlier directive was not unchallenged: Spanish distributors and exhibitors have protested national implementation of the directive and won a positive ruling from the Competition Directorate against a portion of their national law.) In March 1995 Germany's highest court reasserted control by German states over broadcasting and ruled that parts of the EU's 1989 directive were unconstitutional. A compromise forged by the Commission—that quotas should be tightened in the short term and dismantled after ten years—faced continued opposition, and the French government appeared to shift its position toward increasing EU subsidies to the European audio-visual industry.[84]

The Commission compromise, by excluding new television services from the directive, signaled a critical weakness in any protective effort in this sector. The combination of a product highly valued by consumers and rapid technological innovation provides numerous loopholes that may be impossible to close. Cable and satellite television offer means of access to national media markets that are difficult to block. Rules on coproduction are another potential breach in audio-visual policy, since they raise complicated "who is us?" issues. Virtually any rules are likely to be too complex to enforce or, if enforced, will impinge on the interests of a European producer. In this instance, European protective policies, whether based in profound systemic differences or not, are likely to be undermined by a combination of European competitive pressures, consumer demand, and technological change.

Subsidies and technology. State intervention in the economy has been a source of tension between the United States and Europe in sectors other than agriculture and audio-visual. Some core European industries, plagued with overcapacity and often nationalized, have received subsidies that have been challenged by the U.S. government and (through anti-dumping and CVD actions) by American corporations. Steel is a long-running subsidies saga: its latest episodes were played out during the Uruguay Round, when yet another steel war erupted and thwarted efforts to reach a Multilateral Steel Agreement. Trade conflict in steel has been closely related to the business cycle. The recent collapse of the Commission's capacity reduction plan signified that European recovery had reduced economic pressure on weaker members of the industry. Transatlantic conflict is likely to resume with the next recession. Subsidies to state-owned steel companies are becoming more controversial within the EU, however, as privatized and private firms become more competitive, a pattern that characterizes other sectors as well.

Another highly charged subsidies case from the past is the Airbus. The dispute over government support for this challenger to Boeing was dampened by a bilateral aircraft agreement signed in 1992 that imposed disciplines on future European government support for the consortium that has developed Airbus. Efforts to revise the GATT Aircraft Agreement during the Uruguay Round failed, however, and the United States and Europe have continued to negotiate on an expansion of GATT rules in this sector. Although transatlantic conflict may well continue to flare, the enormous cost of research and development in the next generation of projects is forcing American and European aerospace corporations to collaborate. Purely "American" or "European" planes—already a fiction in the generation of Airbus—may become even more chimeric in the next decade.

Conflict over steel subsidies within the EU and the successful conclusion of the 1992 Airbus agreement suggest that subsidies for industry may be of declining importance in future transatlantic trade conflicts. The underlying reasons do not lie in any greater European deference to American views. Rather, since the mid-1980s and the adoption of the Single European Act, scrutiny by the EU of all barriers to European competition, including state aids to industry, has intensified. Recent EU approvals of additional subsidies—to electronics firm Machines Bull, that perennial sink for state assistance, and to a succession of state-owned airlines—has led to claims that the Commission and the EU are once again acquiescing in national support of failing firms. Intense and public conflict within the Commission and the Council of the kind that marked these decisions indicates change, however. It signifies that competition policy is alive and well, and that increasingly powerful interests opposed to state assistance are being heard. The political economy of the two cases was crucial: British Airways and its competitive rivals decided to challenge the approved subsidy to Air France in the European Court. In the case of Machines Bull, the competitive threat to the computer sector came primarily from the United States, not from the failing French firm; as a result, less resistance was voiced to the bailout.[85] Because Europe has become a much more integrated single market, more players, in EU institutions and the European private sector, are inclined to agree that "the greatest insult to a free and single market remains the use of state aid."[86] Added to this procompetitive stance against subsidies is the budgetary stringency introduced by EMU's convergence criteria, which transforms state subsidies into rivals of other, more broadly popular expenditures.

At the same time, there has been some transatlantic convergence in the sensitive area of support by the European Union for technologically advanced "sunrise" industries — those, such as Airbus, that are most likely to cause unease and resistance across the Atlantic. A recent evaluation of European technology policy noted a shift over the last two decades from "fixation with scale" and a belief that European champions could be created from the top down to a more mixed and broader set of European policies that combine support for technological infrastructure, a new emphasis on competition policy, and a broadly welcoming attitude toward inward foreign investment.[87] The new EU industrial policy of the 1990s emphasizes "horizontal" measures of support across sectors and the creation of conditions that will create competitive firms.[88] In "strategic" sectors where the EU perceives itself lagging in a technological race with Japan or the United States, however, it has not forsworn sectoral policies completely. The electronics and information technologies sectors are targeted by several EU programs, for example.[89] Those policies are not designed to produce new "European champions" of the Airbus variety, however. European corporations in these strategic sectors have pressed for EU policies that promote private investment, dismantle monopolies, and deregulate.[90]

Movement away from large-scale sectoral subsidies in the EU has converged on the more modest movement of the Clinton administration toward a friendlier attitude to research

and development subsidies in the Uruguay Round negotiations.[91] The American shift toward industrial policy initiatives is unlikely to survive a Republican Congress. The latest
ideological turn to the right in the United States could revive
transatlantic friction on the issue of subsidies.

The New Trade Agenda: Labor and the Environment

Perhaps the most politically sensitive of the new behind-the-
border issues are those concerning labor standards and the
environment. Their addition to NAFTA was a controversial
step, one that will remain contentious in future trade negotiations in the Western Hemisphere. On this set of issues, however, it is unlikely that the United States and the European
Union often will be on opposing sides. Environmental, labor,
and other regulatory policies may produce conflict in two
ways: higher standards may be challenged as disguised protectionism; lower standards, as social or environmental
dumping. Given the broad similarity of U.S. and European
policies in these domains and the similar pressures within
their political systems to maintain standards, most disputes
have been over charges of disguised protectionism. A recent
dispute that may foreshadow a new range of conflicts in agricultural trade concerns a European ban in 1988 on imports of
beef containing anabolic hormones. Since this embargo affected some U.S. beef exports, the United States retaliated
with a 100 percent tariff on European exports of equivalent
value. Following bilateral discussions, the EC agreed to permit U.S. exporters to ship untreated meat to the European
market. The original ban remains in effect, however.

   As Tim Josling points out, similar issues that link
biotechnology, consumer safety, and agricultural trade are on
the horizon, among them the use of BST and PST as growth
stimulants in livestock and the irradiation of food.[92] Although
technological advances of this kind might be blocked for rea-

sons of economic competition, once again the controversy surrounding these developments on *both* sides of the Atlantic makes it unlikely that they would serve as persistent sources of conflict. Another case that outraged U.S. environmentalists was a GATT panel finding against a U.S. embargo on tuna imports from Mexico. The ban had been authorized by the Marine Mammals Protection Act and was designed to prevent the killing of dolphins in nets that are used in tuna fishing. The original complaint was brought by Mexico; a second GATT panel found against the United States in a second complaint brought by the European Community. From the point of view of the European Union and those who supported its complaint (Canada and Brazil among others), however, this dispute did not concern the environmental ends pursued by the United States. Rather, the EU and other American trading partners saw the legislation in question as yet another attempt to extend American environmental regulation unilaterally through trade sanctions. A similar case that illustrates the difference between European and American positions is an EU ban on the import of furs caught using leg traps. The EU argues that this ban differs from the U.S. ban on Mexican tuna in that the standards applied are international ones, even though the means of enforcement are unilateral rather than multilateral.

Although disputes of this kind are likely to recur, both the United States and the EU will be pressed by environmentalists and labor unions to use market leverage to obtain regulatory harmonization to higher standards. This joint stance was confirmed at the Marrakesh Conference that concluded the Uruguay Round. The European Union and the United States stressed the importance of environmental and labor standards and their linkage to trade on the future WTO agenda. As they have in the past, Europe and the United States are most likely to diverge over the use of unilateral measures to obtain desired policy changes.

System Friction or Economic Conflict?

The array of disputes that has divided the United States and Europe over the past decade does not suggest a deep or growing tension between two alternative political economies. Although the median politician in the United States and the median politician in Europe will still diverge on acceptable levels of state intervention in the economy, the medians have converged, particularly in the era of the 1992 single-market initiative. American unilateralism will still bring European criticisms, as it has in the latest dispute with Japan, but Europe seldom will be the target of that unilateralism. Within EU institutions and within European politics, the balance has shifted toward an emphasis on competition and skepticism regarding targeted state intervention. The fiscal constraints imposed by EMU have only added to this partial convergence. Even in those sectors that display elements of system friction—agriculture and audio-visual—the protective instruments employed have become more controversial, and both technological change and European competitive pressures may erode existing policies further. On other behind-the-border issues at the WTO, such as environmental and labor standards, the EU and the United States typically will be aligned together against a hostile developing country bloc. Transatlantic economic conflicts will continue, particularly if the new WTO mechanisms fail, but those conflicts are unlikely to coalesce into broader, regionalized systemic conflict between the European Union and the United States.

CONCLUSION: REGIONALISM AND TRANSATLANTIC ECONOMIC CONFLICT

A world of old and new regional projects does present the possibility of new conflict between the United States and Europe, but such conflict is unlikely to take the form of interbloc

tensions on the model of the 1930s. The course of regionalization and regional institution-building is uneven; heterogeneity within each region may increase as economic
integration proceeds. The United States, despite its economic
weight within APEC or a Western Hemisphere FTA, is unlikely to forge a common bargaining position from those col-
lections of fiercely sovereign states. Nor is there much sign
that Asia-Pacific or the Western Hemisphere will develop the
institutions and common policies of the European Union.
The European institutional future also remains open, and
many of the alternative paths would ease the dealings of nonmembers with the European Union. The conflicts between
each regional group increasingly will include behind-the-
border issues, but those issues also will *divide* members of
the regions, particularly in the Pacific. The task at hand is to
incorporate the dense network of transatlantic relations, already under some strain since the end of the Cold War, in a
semiregionalized world that must grapple with new sorts of
politically sensitive economic issues.

Regionalism presents the possibility of economic conflict between the United States and Europe, but it does not
subsume all of the sources of friction. Transatlantic alterca-
tions over macroeconomic management and exchange rate
coordination have been persistent since the 1970s. As described earlier, European economic and monetary union may
change that pattern of conflict, but it will not create it. Renewed competition for export contracts in "big emerging
markets" threatens unrestrained mercantilist rivalry in third-
country markets. Although that competition requires negotiated restraint, it is not deepened by regionalism.

New Transatlantic Initiatives

The portrait of transatlantic economic relations given here is
a relatively benign one. Economic conflict is manageable,
and the institutions in place, if they are employed, seem ad-

equate to the task. Nevertheless, unease and anxiety have grown since the end of the Cold War, and a chorus of voices has recommended new transatlantic negotiations and a redefinition of the Atlantic region. The diagnosis that underlies these recommendations often is confused: for some, borrowing realist analysis, the disappearance of the Soviet threat means that some new cement is required to avoid a transatlantic drift apart; others perceive growing economic conflict that could undermine a resilient NATO alliance. The timing of European proposals indicates a high degree of anxiety that the United States may turn its attention away from slow-growing Europe toward Latin America and the Pacific.

Three types of recommendations have been made for the redesign of transatlantic relations. The most familiar is a transatlantic free trade area.[93] A TAFTA would extend the pattern of regionalization observed in Europe, North America, and Asia-Pacific to a new region, the Atlantic. Whether the partners in such an agreement would be NAFTA and the EU or the United States and the EU is unclear; negotiations including the members of NAFTA would be more complicated. Despite the wide ideological spectrum that has endorsed a TAFTA, it is the least attractive of the new transatlantic proposals. Following so soon after the Uruguay Round of global trade negotiations and the formation of the WTO, it is not clear which issues it could address that were not dealt with (or left aside) at the global level. As described earlier, agriculture—now subject to a transatlantic trade truce—is not likely to be revisited successfully; textiles, another sector that is heavily protected, has great political clout in both Europe and the United States. A TAFTA's potential for undermining the global trade regime by establishing such a large discriminatory trading area is serious, as noted in sharp commentary by the new secretary general of the WTO, Renato Ruggiero.[94] The reaction of Asian trading partners is likely to be suspicious or hostile. Finally, a TAFTA often is proposed as a solution to a malaise in NATO and the post–Cold War security relationship between Europe and the United States. However, it is the wrong instrument for resolving those admittedly important security problems.[95]

Sir Leon Brittan, EU commissioner for trade, has proposed a transatlantic "economic area," which, in contrast to a TAFTA, would concentrate on nontariff barriers to trade and investment. Negotiations for an economic area would aim at removing the same types of barriers that were targeted by the European Community's Single European Act, among them competition policy and technical barriers. Brittan has acknowledged the drawbacks to a TAFTA and the limited benefits to tariff elimination; he also has declined to characterize his proposal as a quick fix for reviving the security partnership. The redesign of transatlantic security relations probably will need to await the EU's intergovernmental conference in 1996.[96]

A third set of proposals aims to strengthen ties between the European Union and the United States, moving beyond the 1990 Transatlantic Declaration. The declaration stepped up the level of bilateral consultation between the EU and the U.S. government.[97] The Transatlantic Policy Network recently has proposed adapting and deepening the Transatlantic Declaration framework to further political cooperation between the United States and the European Union. Although disavowing the need for new transatlantic institutions, the TPN does urge the negotiation of a substantive treaty to codify the relationship between the European Union and the United States.

Transatlantic Economic Relations: Introducing a Global Bias

Each of these proposals aims to redesign transatlantic relations in the interest of preserving them. To the degree that they do so by hardening an Atlantic region, they are misguided. This examination of transatlantic economic relations would follow a time-honored tradition if it endorsed one or another of these initiatives in a closing sermonette and proposed a new set of transatlantic institutions to transform relations between these two economic giants. Such new institutions are unnecessary, however, since the European Union and the United States have just spent eight years negotiating a renovated institution that is adequate for many of these purposes: the World Trade Organization. In dealing with the conflicts that will emerge in a world of sometimes competing regional projects, the WTO should be awarded the central role, whether in oversight of those projects and their institutional corollaries or in dealing with the specific behind-the-border differences that spawn economic conflict. If the WTO proves inadequate or if its principal members abandon it, then a second-best institutional solution may be required between the United States and Europe. Transatlantic bilateralism should play an important and complementary role in dealing with those issues that cannot be negotiated efficiently at the global level, in constructing the transnational political underpinnings for the bilateral relationship, and, above all, in providing a means of coordinating U.S.–European collaboration in multilateral settings.

Rethinking international subsidiarity. The United States and the European Union will need to determine whether new issues on their economic agenda will be addressed at the bilateral, regional, or global level. Introducing a principle of global bias into those choices—favoring the global level unless a strong justification can be offered for regional or bilateral negotiation—offers a rule of thumb that would serve to introduce a measure of consistency among regional arrangements and to ensure the central place of global multilateral economic institutions. The development of criteria for assessing which issues should be subject to international scrutiny and which can be dealt with by national governments is equally important for reducing system friction. Elaborating the concept of subsidiarity in other international settings will not offset intense political pressures to define more behind-the-border policies as barriers to market access or sources of "unfair" competitive advantage. Nevertheless, forcing national debates toward some consistency across policies and regions would in itself have considerable value. In addition to this "vertical" subsidiarity, there are important questions of placement *across* international negotiating forums. Whether environmental policies are dealt with in the WTO, for example, makes a clear statement about causal connections across issues.

Monitoring regionalism. As the United States, the European Union, and other members of the world economy create FTAs and customs unions, WTO oversight of regional projects must be strengthened. The revision of GATT Article XXIV in the Uruguay Round was not adequate; the Trade Policy Review Mechanism and biennial reporting requirements for members of regional agreements will increase transparency for nonmembers but not the oversight authority of the WTO.

Defensible criteria for evaluating regional preferential arrangements are difficult to design. John McMillan has suggested one rigorous amendment: explicit compensation for nonmembers in the event of trade diversion (measured against trade volumes before a regional arrangement takes effect). As Robert Lawrence points out, however, there are difficult estimation obstacles both before and after a preferential agreement is implemented. Similar drawbacks weaken other rules to ensure that regional projects serve to liberalize rather than impede economic transactions.[98] The difficulties and ambiguities associated with "open regionalism" were discussed earlier. As Michael Finger suggests, the best WTO convention may be a requirement that members of such arrangements be prepared to negotiate with those whose economic interests are affected. Those affected are likely to be vocal and precise about the features that have disadvantaged them.[99]

An ombudsman for outsiders. Whatever strengthened criteria are developed for WTO oversight of regional arrangements, an international institution is unlikely to criticize the institutional choices made by such groups. As described earlier, however, institutional design may have implications for economic outcomes and for a regional group's future international behavior. The appointment of a panel to report on the implications of institutional choices for nonmembers is one solution to the inward-looking bias of regional institution-building. Such an ombudsman for outsiders should be nongovernmental and should not be cast as a partisan for or against a regional project. Each major regional organization could, as a sign of its own good intentions and its commitment to transparency, appoint such an ombudsman panel, provide resources for its work, and publicize its findings.

Negotiating behind-the-border issues. The future transatlantic economic agenda will be dominated by issues that were once defined as "domestic." Many of those issues can be negotiated within the World Trade Organization. The GATT/WTO, despite delays in completing the Uruguay Round, has demonstrated valuable flexibility in meeting the new agenda of behind-the-border issues and containing conflicts between the United States and the European Community.

The incorporation of new agenda items into the multilateral negotiating system has become a two-step process. For many issues, the Organization for Economic Cooperation and Development has played a valuable, if almost invisible, initial role in establishing common vocabulary, benchmarks, and standards of measurement in a setting that does not immediately involve binding agreements. Those understandings may then move to the broader membership, binding obligations, and dispute settlement mechanism of the WTO. Prospective expansion of the OECD to include industrializing economies will make it an even more useful testing ground for issues that are not ready for the WTO agenda.

Embedding the United States and the European Union in such a global and multilateral network has several important benefits. First, the presence of other members, of increasing importance in their own right, does affect the negotiating behavior of these economic behemoths. The Cairns Group of agricultural exporters helped at critical points to keep the Uruguay Round negotiations on track; this is only one example of the beneficial role that outsiders can play in moderating transatlantic economic disputes. Transatlantic relations in multilateral settings will benefit from such external scrutiny and participation. Second, global institutions provide an avenue for incorporating new international economic actors on a nonpreferential basis. Discriminatory and exclusive dealings can breed distrust between the United States and Europe: the MFN principle incorporated in the WTO places their relations with a growing list of trading powers on an equal footing.

These new trading powers should be included at an early stage in international economic negotiations; their inclusion is engineered most easily in global negotiations. This logic of extension was apparent in the preparations for new negotiations on international rules governing investment. Although this issue—perhaps the most important on the international economic agenda—has been proposed for a bilateral U.S.–European Union accord, the United States and the European Union agreed that the negotiations should take place in a wider setting. Sir Leon Brittan and the Commission favored the WTO; the United States pressed for the OECD. Regional or bilateral settings were regarded as distinctly second best.[100]

Successfully incorporating transatlantic economic relations in global multilateral regimes depends on the investment that the European Union and the United States will make in those institutions. Given its important economic ties to several regions, the United States has a strong interest in a credible multilateral trade regime. Despite past European skepticism about the GATT and prospective enlargement of the EU, Europe also may display new interest in the WTO. Slow economic growth in the 1990s and a declining share of world exports suggest that the positive effects of deepening European integration were overestimated and the benefits of opening to rapidly expanding regions in Latin America and East and Southeast Asia ignored. Given the obstacles to further enlargement in the short run, a multilateral strategy of reciprocal opening to dynamic producers outside the region may produce more benefits for the EU.

These two trading giants have employed the GATT dispute settlement mechanism (DSM) in the past, but their compliance with panel decisions has been poor. In the history of GATT, over 90 percent of the complaints have involved either the United States or the European Community (or its members) as a party.[101] The EC became a more frequent complainant in the 1980s, and the United States (during the era of aggressive unilateralism) was a prominent target of complaints.[102] For the new organization to succeed, the EU and the United States must employ the strengthened DSM of the WTO and abide by unfavorable decisions. Despite U.S. eagerness to obtain a strengthened DSM, its recent record of compliance, the oversight demanded and obtained by the U.S. Senate before ratification, and the unilateralism evident in its automobile dispute with Japan do not augur well for global management of transatlantic disputes.

Bilateral Economic Relations in a New Era

Although transatlantic economic relations should be embedded in a multilateral framework and the creation of yet another region with its own institutions is unnecessary, deepening the bilateral relationship remains complementary to and perhaps essential for a global partnership. The United States and the European Union should concentrate on three fields of cooperation: preempting system friction by innovative negotiations on behind-the-border issues; strengthening the political base of the relationship by fostering transnational coalitions; and constructing a means of bilateral collaboration and leadership within multilateral institutions and negotiations. These three cooperative strategies appear in many of the recent transatlantic proposals.

Innovation in bilateral economic relations. Maintaining the extensive network of bilateral economic ties between the European Union and the United States remains important; a free trade area is not necessary for that purpose. Since 1989 the Bush and Clinton administrations have sought actively to strengthen a range of consultations at the cabinet and sub-cabinet levels. Perhaps the most useful role that bilateral economic negotiations can play, however, is experimentation and innovation in negotiating behind-the-border issues. Even if negotiations are biased toward global institutions such as the WTO and OECD, certain issues will be negotiated more efficiently as part of a transatlantic agenda. The transatlantic relationship has produced particular advantages: a high level of transparency in policymaking and deep economic integration through cross-investment.

Strategies of mutual recognition and regulatory harmonization may work between the European Union and the United States, although they are unlikely to succeed among negotiating partners whose relations are less close. The

United States and the European Union have initiated a dialogue on regulatory cooperation aimed at increasing both transparency and mutual understanding of regulatory goals, which often may appear protectionist to those seeking market access. In the biotechnology and information technology sectors, in particular, regulatory frameworks change rapidly to match swift technological change. Regulatory agencies continue to define their roles in domestic terms and to respond to domestic demands. Regulatory cooperation between the United States and the EU serves to introduce the trade and investment consequences of regulatory action to the regulators. An initiative on mutual recognition for conformity assessment is more advanced: it would permit firms in Europe and the United States to seek assessment of conformity to standards in the other's market through testing in their own laboratories. Such an agreement would not include harmonization of standards; it would, however, relieve a burdensome set of regulatory procedures for firms on either side of the Atlantic. Finally, regular subcabinet consultations have adopted an early warning system to flag disputes that could develop into full-blown trade conflicts.[103]

Such innovations will resolve or preempt certain transatlantic economic conflicts; institutions with wider membership may adopt them later as useful templates. To deal with other corrosive and long-running issues, such as agriculture, a different set of strategies must be deployed. One is, simply, patience. Technological change and the shifting perceptions of interest that it brings may be enough to undermine objectionable policies: such a process ultimately may shift EU policies toward the audio-visual sector. A key question as economic integration proceeds within the European Union and across the Atlantic is whether integration will produce institutional convergence. The answer so far is clear: not in all circumstances. Some institutions are sheltered from the pressures of integration; others are tightly linked to more resilient institutions.

One barrier to change, however, is lack of reliable information about the effects of particular policies. That information may confirm perceptions of interests; in many cases, however, new knowledge also may begin the redefinition of interests. The creation and dissemination of new knowledge may well be the best strategy for irreducible and long-standing conflicts. The role of the OECD in producing policy convergence on agriculture—at least permitting a common definition of terms and conditions—is an exemplar of this process. Further redefinition of agricultural policies as regional or environmental policies may be required before the political deadlock on this issue can be broken. Much of the concern over the trade and environment link might be allayed with additional information: for example, the lack of evidence for environmental dumping. Intellectual naïveté is not justified, however, since some issues are driven by political and ideological dynamics that are impervious to argument and information. Institutional transfer to support convergence may be difficult. Nevertheless, while waiting for economic change, the political landscape may be changed, one stone at a time, by encouraging a process of transatlantic learning and supporting the transfer of best practice from one side of the Atlantic to the other.

Encouraging transnational alliances. One of the greatest assets in the management of transatlantic economic relations—in contrast to U.S.–Japan economic relations—is the high level of cross-investment in the two economies. Every effort should be made to encourage this feature of the relationship, since it shifts the incentives for those who manage transatlantic economic conflict and provides a powerful stabilizing element. Foreign investors may induce conflict by encouraging their home governments to take up real or imagined competitive disadvantages that are imposed in the host country or region. They also may be co-opted into local cartels and preferential arrangements. More frequently, particularly in global production networks, they create difficult "who is us?" problems for governments that view a particular conflict in purely territorial and national (or European) terms. The aircraft industry, the source of many hours of negotiation and much high-level confrontation between the United States and Europe, is a case in point. One recent estimate of this "murky and incestuous world" is that about half of any Airbus by value will go to American suppliers.[104] If those linked interests become politically active, efforts to frame the issue in a purely us-against-them fashion are more likely to be undermined. Cross-investors also produce reliable allies for policies maintaining openness, given the trend of transatlantic liberalization during the post-1945 decades.

Recent transatlantic initiatives have called for institutionalizing U.S.–European Union business representation and collaboration. Given the power of existing business organizations, such institutionalization is probably less necessary than the fostering of other transnational ties. The scope of transnational alliance-building needs to reach beyond the corporate sector. One potential threat to transatlantic relations is the growing belief that international economic integration is managed by a cabal of governments and corporations to the exclusion of other interests, such as labor, consumers, and the environment. These latter groups must be included in setting the transatlantic economic agenda. The processes of economic diplomacy necessarily will be opened: the WTO already has felt intense pressure in this regard. There are risks in such an opening: the processes must be managed to ensure that they are not captured by groups that are unrepresentative. Nevertheless, whether governments like it or not, the active management of a widened transatlantic diplomacy will become a central feature of the new international politics between Europe and the United States.

Virtually every study of economic diplomacy and the exercise of international influence—whether programs of the

International Monetary Fund, economic sanctions, or "aggressive unilateralism"—confirms that success is highly correlated with the existence of tacit or explicit allies in the domestic political economy of the target state or region.[105] The European Union and the United States occasionally have played on such interests to considerable effect; the development of such "constituencies" on an issue-by-issue basis should be a major part of transatlantic diplomacy as its agenda shifts toward more sensitive and politically entrenched issues. Such appeals may well be condemned as "meddling" or "splitting the Union" by those who would prefer their political hand to be played in a less complicated setting, but in a highly integrated economy, such political strategies may be the most effective and, in the long run, the most beneficial.

Success in Transatlantic Relations

Many analyses of transatlantic relations start with a real or imagined crisis and end with anodyne recommendations for bilateral band-aids. Recent proposals for new transatlantic initiatives and institutions are more ambitious, but their criteria for success remain the dampening of conflicts and the maintenance of what is seen to be a sturdy and valuable element in international politics. Unfortunately, such a low benchmark for "success" may be inadequate for the future. A revived transatlantic relationship must aim at joint action in the global tasks that confront the United States and the European Union. Such shared goals as incorporating the former Soviet bloc into international economic regimes, preventing the marginalization of parts of the developing world, and devising collective and efficient means to deal with environmental issues require positive collaborative action. That collaboration will take place, however, in a global setting that awards the European Union and the United States only a temporary and rapidly eroding economic dominance. Perhaps the most startling developments of the 1980s and 1990s have been the rapid spread of policies that link previously closed economies to the world economy and the very high levels of economic growth that have resulted in many parts of the industrializing world. East and Southeast Asia are prime examples; the process and the results are far more fragile and uneven in South Asia and Latin America.

In many areas of economic diplomacy, the United States and Europe, and even the United States, Europe, and Japan as a bloc, have become a necessary but not a sufficient core coalition for accomplishing global ends. A bipolar or tripolar world might be more conflictual, but it also could provide a means of organizing collective action. Such clear tripolarity is unlikely, however, for the reasons given earlier. Instead, a pattern of changing, issue-based international coalitions will characterize international economic relations. The Uruguay Round was a first signal of the new pattern. The once potent North-South divide eroded under the impact of new policy choices in the developing world. The divide between communist and non-communist coalitions also has disappeared. Renewed interest in regional arrangements is yet another sign of this new pattern of diversification and linkage in the international economy. In their international economic relations, few countries will rely entirely on a regional strategy (or a purely global or unilateral strategy).

The need for the United States and Europe to manage such a complex pattern of interests adds a final reason for strengthening global institutions when possible and ensuring the mutual consistency of regional efforts. These common global goals also pose the need for better means of "bilateral concertation on multilateral issues" between the United States and the European Union.[106] Constructing a new transatlantic region through an FTA would not guarantee such concerted action; whatever its benign intent, it could well create resistance by the nations that need to be incorporated in global coalitions and institutions.

Whatever economic conflicts ensue between the transatlantic economic powers, the European Union and the United States will remain essential to any global bargains that are reached. On most global economic issues, they will continue to share many of the same goals. Their shared core interests will become even clearer as their joint position relative to the rest of the world diminishes. Although Europe and the United States now cohabit a world that is far less threatening and far more representative of their values than the world of only a few decades ago, the changes that have produced that more benign environment are hardly secure. The joint task of the EU and the United States is to craft a structure of governance that is sturdy enough to lock those changes into place and flexible enough to accommodate the surprises and ruptures that always will characterize our heterogeneous planet.

NOTES

1. For a sharply etched analysis of this kind, see John J. Mearsheimer, "Back to the Future: Instability in Europe after the Cold War," *International Security* 15, no. 1 (Summer 1990), pp. 5–56.
2. Lester Thurow, *Head to Head: The Coming Economic Battle among Japan, Europe, and America* (New York: Morrow, 1992).
3. Wayne Sandholtz et al., *The Highest Stakes: The Economic Foundations of the Next Security System* (New York: Oxford University Press, 1992), pp. 197–199.
4. In *Allies, Adversaries, and International Trade* (Princeton, NJ: Princeton University Press, 1994). Joanne Gowa has argued that trade patterns follow military alliances.
5. This argument is made in greater detail in Miles Kahler, "Revision and Prevision: Historical Interpretation and the Future of Transatlantic Relations," in Miles Kahler and Werner Link, *Europe and America at the Dawn of a New Era: A Return of History* (New York: Council on Foreign Relations Press, 1995).
6. This section is based on a more complete account in Miles Kahler, "A World of Blocs: Facts and Factoids," *World Policy Journal* 12, no. 1 (Spring 1995), pp. 19–27.
7. For a discussion of this distinction, see Albert Fishlow and Stephan Haggard, *The United States and the Regionalization of the World Economy* (Paris: OECD, 1992), pp. 12–14.
8. On these results and issues of measurement, see Jeffrey A. Frankel, "Is Japan Creating a Yen Bloc in East Asia and the Pacific?" in Jeffrey A. Frankel and Miles Kahler, eds., *Regionalism and Rivalry* (Chicago: University of Chicago Press, 1993), pp. 54–66.
9. For an assessment of this possibility, see Richard F. Doner, "Japanese Foreign Investment and the Creation of a Pacific Asian Region," in Frankel and Kahler, eds., *Regionalism and Rivalry*, pp. 159–214.
10. Margaret R. Kelly and Augusto de la Torre, *Regional Trade Arrangements* (Washington, D.C.: International Monetary Fund, 1992), p. 13.

11. In a speech to the third Euro-Latin American Forum (July 7, 1994), GATT Director-General Peter Sutherland noted that "the conclusion that the world is witnessing the creation of three inward-oriented 'trading blocs,' based in North America, in Western Europe and in the Asia-Pacific region is not supported by an analysis of trends in the pattern of world trade." *GATT/WTO News*, July 7, 1994, p. 5.

12. On these and other grounds, Jagdish Bhagwati remains a prominent critic of "the infatuation with FTAs." See "U.S. Trade Policy: The Infatuation with FTAs," in Claude Barfield, ed., *The Dangerous Drift to Preferential Trade* (Washington, D.C.: American Enterprise Institute, 1995).

13. Robert Z. Lawrence, *Regionalism, Multilateralism and Deeper Integration* (Washington, D.C.: Brookings Institution, 1995).

14. "Plurilateral" describes an international arrangement or grouping that has more than two but substantially less than universal membership. Its members may or may not be geographically proximate.

15. For a summary of the changes in Reagan administration trade policy, see Thomas O. Bayard and Kimberly Ann Elliott, *Reciprocity and Retaliation in U.S. Trade Policy* (Washington, D.C.: Institute for International Economics, 1994), pp. 15–19.

16. The regional distribution of American trade and investment interests is summarized in Stephan Haggard, "Thinking About Regionalism: The Politics of Minilateralism in Asia and the Americas." Paper presented at the Annual Meetings of the American Political Science Association, New York, September 1994, pp. 19–20.

17. A detailed account of the NAFTA agreement is given in Gary Clyde Hufbauer and Jeffrey J. Schott, *NAFTA: An Assessment* (Washington, D.C.: Institute for International Economics, 1993).

18. For a skeptical view of the NAFTA strategy, see Stephan Haggard, "The United States and Regionalism in Asia and the Americas," in *Asia-Pacific and the Americas: Reconciling Regional and Global Economic Interests* (La Jolla, CA: Institute of the Americas, 1994), pp. 20–23; for an endorsement of hemispheric integration through widening of NAFTA, see Gary Clyde Hufbauer and Jeffrey J. Schott, *Western Hemisphere Economic Integration* (Washington, D.C.: Institute for International Economics, 1994), pp. 176–182.

19. This option has been proposed jointly by the Organization of American States, the Inter-American Development Bank, and the Economic Commission for Latin America and the Caribbean; see *CEPAL News* 14, no. 11 (November 1994).

20. That seems an implicit assumption of Hufbauer and Schott, *Western Hemisphere Economic Integration*.

21. C. Fred Bergsten, "Sunrise in Seattle," *International Economic Insights* 5, no. 1 (January/February 1994), pp. 18–20.

22. The first EPG report was published as *A Vision for APEC: Towards an Asia Pacific Economic Community* (1993).
23. The second EPG report was published as *Achieving the APEC Vision: Free and Open Trade in the Asia Pacific* (1994).
24. On the other hand, Malaysia continued unilateral liberalization of its own trade regime and agreed to host the 1998 APEC summit.
25. On the likely effects of a Western Hemisphere FTA, for example, see Hufbauer and Schott, *Western Hemisphere Economic Integration*, pp. 162–166.
26. Commission of the European Communities, *EC/US Relations: Progress Report* 2 (December 1, 1993), p. 11.
27. C. Fred Bergsten and C. Randall Henning, "Europe's Role in the World Economy: An American View." Paper presented to the joint conference of the Institute for International Economics and Austrian National Bank, "Europe: What Next?" October 18–19, 1993, Vienna, Austria, p. 33.
28. On competitive liberalization versus competitive regionalization, see Jeffrey A. Frankel and Shang-Jin Wei, "European Integration and the Regionalization of World Trade and Currencies: The Economics and the Politics," ms., February 1995, pp. 31–34.
29. An excellent account of the Mexican crisis and its transatlantic dimension is given in George Graham et al., "Bitter Legacy of Battle to Bail Out Mexico," *Financial Times*, February 16, 1995, p. 4.
30. For example, Mark M. Nelson, "Transatlantic Travails," *Foreign Policy* 92 (Fall 1993), p. 87.
31. Bayard and Elliott, *Reciprocity and Retaliation*, pp. 297–298.
32. Bergsten and Henning, "Europe's Role in the World Economy," pp. 20, 24.
33. Mark M. Nelson and G. John Ikenberry, *Atlantic Frontiers: A New Agenda for U.S.-EC Relations* (Washington, D.C.: Carnegie Endowment for International Peace, 1993), pp. 19–20; see also Robert B. Zoellick's preface to this report, in which he argues that the U.S. "should be increasingly discriminating about the content, form, and resulting outlook of the EC" (p. vii).
34. Nelson and Ikenberry, *Atlantic Frontiers*, p. 24.
35. On the importance of transparency for multilateral commitments, see Peter F. Cowhey, "Domestic Institutions and the Credibility of International Commitments: Japan and the United States," *International Organization* 47, no. 2 (Spring 1993), pp. 301–302.
36. Fabio Luca Cavazza and Carlo Pelanda, "Maastricht: Before, During, After," *Daedalus* 123, no. 2 (Spring 1994), p. 58; Richard Corbett, *The Treaty of Maastricht* (London: Longman Group UK Ltd., 1993), p. 62.

37. Lionel Barber, "Opportunity for Fine-tuning," *Financial Times*, May 10, 1995, p. 13.

38. Corbett, *Treaty of Maastricht*, p. 39.

39. See Lionel Barber, "EU Single Currency 'Unlikely before 2002,'" *Financial Times*, April 10, 1995, p. 1; Julie Wolf, "EC Monetary-Union Timetable Delays Common Currency Until Next Century," *Wall Street Journal*, May 30, 1995, p. A9F.

40. John Forsyth, "The ECU, the Dollar and the Yen," in C. A. E. Goodhart, *EMU and ESCB After Maastricht* (London: Financial Markets Group, 1992), p. 313.

41. Peter Kenen, "EMU after Maastricht," in Goodhart, *EMU and ESCB*, p. 165.

42. Charles Goodhart, "The External Dimension of EMU," in Goodhart, *EMU and ESCB*, p. 328.

43. C. Randall Henning, *Currencies and Politics in the United States, Germany, and Japan* (Washington, D. C.: Institute for International Economics, 1994), p. 365.

44. Kenen, "EMU after Maastricht," p. 165.

45. For alternative definitions of and remedies for the democratic deficit, see Lisa Martin, "Economic and Political Integration: Institutional Challenge and Response." Paper presented at the conference "The Political Economy of European Integration: The Challenges Ahead," April 20–22, 1995, Berkeley, CA.

46. For example, in a vote on liberalization of telecommunications, the Parliament pressed for broadening the scope of the legislation; on ending national railway monopolies, the European Parliament backed the Commission against dilution in the Council of Ministers. *Eurowatch* 7, no. 3 (April 1995), p. 3.

47. This point was made by European participants in the ECSA/TEPSA seminar in Brussels.

48. On this point, see Cowhey, "Domestic Institutions."

49. Andrew Moravscik, "Why the European Community Strengthens the State: Domestic Politics and International Cooperation," Center for European Studies, Working Paper Series 52, pp. 56–57.

50. Lisa L. Martin, "The Influence of National Parliaments on European Integration," Center for International Affairs, Harvard University, Working Paper 94–10, December 1994.

51. Kees van Kersbergen and Bertjan Verbeek, "The Politics of Subsidiarity in the European Union," *Journal of Common Market Studies* 32, no. 2 (June 1994), pp. 215–236.

52. David Begg et al., *Making Sense of Subsidiarity: How Much Centralization for Europe?* (London: Center for Economic Policy Research, 1993), p. 13.

53. The CEPR study, for example, suggests that the principle of subsidiarity would award agriculture to the national level.

54. Lionel Barber, "Positive Vote for a Bigger Club," *Financial Times*, November 15, 1994, p. 17.

55. Richard E. Baldwin, *Towards an Integrated Europe* (London: Center for Economic Policy Research, 1994), pp. 182–183.

56. Alberta Sbragia, "Asymmetrical Integration in the European Community: The Single European Act and Institutional Development" in Dale L. Smith and Jame Lee Ray, eds., *The 1992 Project and the Future of Integration in Europe* (Armonk, NY: M. E. Sharpe, 1993), p. 93.

57. Ibid.

58. Fritz Scharpf, "The Joint-Decision Trap: Lessons from German Federalism and European Integration," *Public Administration* 66 (Autumn 1988), pp. 239–278.

59. Following the defeat of the Maastricht Treaty in the Danish referendum, the special arrangements for Denmark were expanded.

60. For the most complete argument along these lines, see Baldwin, *Towards an Integrated Europe*.

61. Per Magnus Wijkman, "EFTA Countries," in C. Randall Henning and Eduard Hochreiter, eds., *Reviving the European Union* (Washington, D.C.: Institute for International Economics, 1994), p. 93. Wijkman urges the EFTA as a halfway house; Baldwin proposes an Association of Association Agreements and an Organization for European Integration.

62. Michael Smith and Stephen Woolcock, "Learning to Cooperate: The Clinton Administration and the European Union," *International Affairs* 70, no. 3 (July 1994), pp. 459–476. Smith and Woolcock refer to the work of Michel Albert, *Capitalisme contre capitalisme* (Paris: Seuil, 1992), who makes this argument at greater length.

63. Stanley Hoffmann, "Europe's Identity Crisis Revisited," *Daedalus* 123, no. 2 (Spring 1994), p. 14.

64. A more detailed account of the setting of this new agenda is given in Miles Kahler, "Trade and Domestic Differences," in Suzanne Berger and Ronald Dore, eds., *Convergence or Diversity?: National Models of Production and Distribution in a Global Economy* (Ithaca, NY: Cornell University Press, forthcoming).

65. Perhaps the best example of negotiations on the new issues to date was the Structural Impediments Initiative negotiations between the United States and Japan.

66. Suzanne Berger and Ronald Dore, "Convergence or Diversity?: National Models of Production and Distribution in a Global Economy," in Berger and Dore, eds., *Convergence or Diversity?*

67. A recent summary is given in *Report on US Barriers to Trade and Investment* (Brussels: Services of the European Commission, April 1994), pp. 3–6.

68. The European bill of particulars is given in ibid.; that of the United States in U.S. Office of the Trade Representative, *National Trade Estimate Report on Foreign Trade Barriers* (Washington, D.C.: Government Printing Office, 1994).

69. Pietro Nivola documents this shift in American trade policy in *Regulating Unfair Trade* (Washington, D.C.: Brookings Institution, 1993), pp. 21, 24–25.

70. "Super" 301 authorized the USTR to identify unfair trading countries; "special" 301 targeted inadequate protection of intellectual property rights. An excellent account of the evolution of Section 301 is given in Bayard and Elliott, *Reciprocity and Retaliation*, ch. 2.

71. Ibid., pp. 60–61. Figures cited are for the period 1975 to 1993. In the 1990 to 1993 period all 301 cases directed against Europe concerned agriculture.

72. Guy de Jonquières, "Fears Grow that EU's Weapon May Misfire," *Financial Times*, November 29, 1994, p.6.

73. Lionel Barber, "Brussels Reaches for a Tougher Trade Weapon," *Financial Times*, October 27, 1994, p. 4.

74. Kym Anderson, "Trade Negotiations and Farm Policy," *Economic Policy* 18 (April 1994), pp. 14–52.

75. For an account of these negotiations, see Charles Iceland, "European Union: Oilseeds," in Bayard and Elliott, *Reciprocity and Retaliation*, ch. 9; Anderson, "Trade Negotiations," pp. 28–33.

76. Tim Josling, "Agricultural Trade Issues in Transatlantic Trade Relations," *The World Economy* 16, no. 5 (September 1993), pp. 557–558.

77. Results are summarized in Anderson, "Trade Negotiations," p. 32; the full text is given in *The Results of the Uruguay Round of Multilateral Trade Negotiations: The Legal Texts* (Geneva: GATT, 1994), pp. 39–68.

78. Anderson, "Trade Negotiations," p. 28; Josling, "Agricultural Trade Issues," pp. 571–572; L. Alan Winters, "Comment," in Anderson, "Trade Negotiations," p. 48.

79. "The Development and Future of the Common Agricultural Policy," *Bulletin of the European Communities*, Supplement 5 (1991), p. 12.

80. Susan Carol Rogers, "Farming Visions: Culture and Agriculture in France," paper prepared for presentation at the Program in Agrarian Studies, Yale University, November 4, 1994; "Good to Think: The 'Peasant' in Contemporary France," *Anthropological Quarterly* 60, no. 2 (April 1987), pp. 56–63.

81. A London newspaper in the interwar years warned that "The film is to America what the flag was once to Britain. By its means Uncle Sam may hope some day, if he be not checked in time, to Americanize the world." Cited in Frank Costigliola, *Awkward Dominion: American Political, Economic, and Cultural Relations with Europe, 1919–1933* (Ithaca, NY: Cornell University Press, 1984).

82. Philip R. Schlesinger, "Europe's Contradictory Communicative Space," *Daedalus* 123, no. 2 (Spring 1994), pp. 33–34.

83. Ibid., p. 39.

84. Accounts of the evolution of EU policy are given in Emma Tucker, "Brussels in New Fights to Protect European Culture, *Financial Times,* February 9, 1995, p. 1; Emma Tucker, "France Launches New Call for Quotas on US Films and TV," *Financial Times*, February 14, 1995, p. 16; Caroline Southey et al., "Brussels Agrees Deal for Tighter Film and TV Quotas," *Financial Times*, March 23, 1995, p. 1; Alan Riding, "New Curbs Proposed on Foreign TV Programs in Europe," *New York Times*, March 23, 1995, p. D8.

85. "Mad Bull Disease," *The Economist*, October 15, 1994, pp. 67–68.

86. "Family Frictions," *The Economist*, October 22, 1994, p. 16.

87. Margaret Sharp and Keith Pavitt, "Technology Policy in the 1990s: Old Trends and New Realities," *Journal of Common Market Studies* 31, no. 2 (June 1993), pp. 137, 139.

88. Phedon Nicolaides, "Industrial Policy: The Problem of Reconciling Definitions, Intentions and Effects" and Pierre Buigues and André Sapir, "Industrial Policy in an Integrated European Economy," in Phedon Nicolaides, ed., *Industrial Policy in the European Community* (Dordrecht: Martinus Nijhoff Publishers, 1993), pp. 1–20, 21–38.

89. On the development of those programs in response to international competition, see Wayne Sandholtz, *High-Tech Europe: The Politics of International Cooperation* (Berkeley: University of California Press, 1992).

90. Most strikingly in the *Report of the High-Level Group on the Information Society, Europe and the Global Information Society: Recommendations to the European Council*, Brussels, May 26, 1994.

91. See Richard Steinberg, "The Uruguay Round: A Legal Analysis of the Final Act," *International Quarterly* 6, no. 2 (April 1994), pp. 31–32.

92. Josling, "Agricultural Trade Issues," p. 567.

93. A TAFTA has been suggested by the EU ambassador to the United States, Dries van Agt *(Washington Post*, November 18, 1994, p. B1); by the Canadian prime minister, Jean Chrétien; by the U.S. undersecretary of commerce, Jeffrey Garten; and by Lane Kirkland, head of the A.F.L.-C.I.O., among others. U.S. Secretary of State Warren

Christopher has stated that the United States will give the idea of a TAFTA "the serious study it deserves," but has not endorsed the idea. "Charting a Transatlantic Agenda for the 21st Century: Address by Secretary of State Warren Christopher," Casa de America, Madrid, Spain, June 2, 1995.

94. Guy de Jonquières, "Warning on EU-US Free Trade Area," *Financial Times*, April 24, 1995, p. 6.

95. Commentary on the TAFTA proposal is given in "In Need of Fastening," *The Economist*, May 27, 1995, pp. 15–16; Thomas J. Duesterberg, "Prospects for an EU-NAFTA Free Trade Agreement," *The Washington Quarterly* 18, no. 2 (Spring 1995), pp. 71–82; Nathaniel C. Nash, "Is a Trans-Atlantic Pact Coming Down the Pike?" *New York Times*, April 15, 1995, p. 32; "Priorities in World Trade," *Financial Times*, April 28, 1995, p. 13; Lionel Barber and Guy de Jonquières, "US and Europe Eye Each Other Up," *Financial Times*, May 12, 1995, p. 2.

96. James Pressley, "EU Trade Chief Aims to Bolster Ties with U. S.," *Wall Street Journal*, April 28, 1995, p. B4B; Lionel Barber, "Brittan Supports Overhaul of EU-US Relations," *Financial Times*, April 28, 1995, p. 2. Brittan's suggestion was echoed by Swedish Foreign Trade and EU Affairs Minister Mats Hellström. See Guy de Jonquières, "Sweden Urges End to EU-US Non-Tariff Barriers," *Financial Times*, May 3, 1995, p. 6.

97. On the negotiation and implications of the Transatlantic Declaration, see Kevin Featherstone and Roy H. Ginsberg, eds., *The United States and the European Community in the 1990s: Partners in Transition* (New York: St. Martin's Press, 1993), pp. 90–95.

98. Lawrence, *Regionalism, Multilateralism, and Deeper Integration*.

99. J. Michael Finger, "GATT's Influence on Regional Arrangements," in Jaime de Melo and Arvind Panagariya, eds., *New Dimensions in Regional Integration* (Cambridge: Cambridge University Press, 1993), p. 145.

100. Investment rules are part of the transatlantic agenda proposed in Nelson and Ikenberry, *Atlantic Frontiers*, pp. 15–17.

101. Robert E. Hudec, Daniel L. M. Kennedy, and Mark Sgarbossa, "A Statistical Profile of GATT Dispute Settlement Cases: 1948–1989," *Minnesota Journal of Global Trade* 2, no. 1 (Winter 1993), p. 30.

102. Ibid., pp. 34–35.

103. *EU/US Relations: Progress Report on EU-US Relations* (July 1994), p. 11; (December 1994), pp. 6, 9–10.

104. "Family Frictions," *The Economist*, October 22, 1994, p. 9.

105. One excellent study of a recent case is the Structural Impediments Initiative with Japan, see Leonard J. Schoppa, "Two-level Games and Bargaining Outcomes: Why Gaiatsu Succeeds in Japan in Some

Cases but Not Others," *International Organization* 47, no. 3 (Summer 1993), pp. 353–386.

106. Transatlantic Policy Network, *Toward Transatlantic Partnership: A European Strategy* (Brussels; 1994), p. 9.

INDEX

ABOUT THE AUTHOR

Miles Kahler is senior fellow for international political economy at the Council on Foreign Relations and professor of international relations at the Graduate School of International Relations and Pacific Studies, University of California, San Diego. His recent publications include *Regionalism and Rivalry: Japan and the U.S. in Pacific Asia* (co-editor) and *International Institutions and the Political Economy of Integration*. Professor Kahler is chair of the editorial board of *International Organization* and a member of the editorial board of *World Politics*. He has been chair of the Committee on Foreign Policy Studies of the Social Science Research Council and currently serves as a member of the Executive Committee of the Program for International Studies in Asia.